Extravagant Love

EXPLORING GOD'S PASSION
FOR US

Carole Engle Avriett

SALEM
BOOKS
an imprint of Regnery Publishing
Washington, D.C.

Cataloging-in-Publication data on file with the Library of Congress.
ISBN: 978-1-68451-348-2
eISBN: 978-1-68451-399-4

Published in the United States by
Salem Books
An Imprint of Regnery Publishing
A Division of Salem Media Group
Washington, D.C.
www.SalemBooks.com

Manufactured in the United States of America

10 9 8 7 6 5 4 3 2 1

Books are available in quantity for promotional or premium use. For information on discounts and terms, please visit our website: www.SalemBooks.com.

Praise for
Extravagant Love

"*Extravagant Love* causes the reader to pause for a moment and examine God's heart in an easy-to-read, conversational manner. It calls us to consider the intricacies of His relationship with us while sparking deep appreciation for the selfless love He showers us with daily. Be ready for a guided journey to God's heart. As Carole's pastor for eleven years, I had a front-row seat to her journey. She has experienced, and is an exceptional ambassador of, His extravagant love."

   —**David F. Uth,** PhD, senior pastor of First Baptist Church, Orlando, Florida

"The first time I heard Carole Avriett tell one of the stories she includes in *Extravagant Love* was at a women's conference. Captivated by her powerful word pictures, I found myself envisioning a painting of Jesus lingering on a Galilean hillside, watching over every one of His followers until they were safely home. It was a beautiful word picture from Mark 6 that mentally and permanently etched for me magnificent and tender thoughts of the love of our Lord! Whether Carole is speaking or writing, you can expect excellence, truth, and good stories with unforgettable word pictures. *Extravagant Love* is no exception!"

   —**Jackie Bobbitt,** former women's ministry director of Englewood Baptist Church, Jackson, Tennessee

"Carole Avriett provides a wealth of illustration, insight, and application that draws the reader to the reality of God's heart: His desire for relationship with the people He created. This is a gold mine for the academic and the devotional reader."

   —**Jim Henry,** DMin, pastor emeritus of First Baptist Church, Orlando, Florida, and former president of the Southern Baptist Convention

Extravagant Love

Dedicated to my Dad, whose strong prayers helped save me

CONTENTS

Author's Note

C. S. Lewis once said, "You ask for a loving God: you have one."[1] He goes on to say that God's love is passionate and exacting like a lover's: jealous, perhaps even overbearing at times. I can't remember ever writing a manuscript where I had to stop so many times and just take a few moments to soak in what it means for God to love me in such remarkable ways.

Here is what I have prayed over every page of this book: that as you read each word and sentence, God's love will become so real to you that it will fill every crevice of your heart—even the ones you thought could never be filled or mended. You are indeed loved, my friend, and the One who loves you is the King Himself.

Introduction

Most of us go through that awkward stage between girlhood and blossoming into young women when we think we will be resigned forever to living in the basement just like Cinderella. Oddly, though we understand her plight on the inside, we think we resemble the ugly stepsisters on the outside.

At least that's how we may feel. I know I did. Entering my teenage years, I possessed two left feet, "eye teeth" growing way up in my gumline, unmanageable hair, the occasional pimples, an overabundance of hair growing on my arms and legs, and nearly zero confidence that life would ever get any better.

Until one day . . . my dad gave me something. He had been away on a shoe-buying trip to St. Louis with his bosses. My parents were hardworking clothing salespeople, putting in six days a week with little money left over for extras. We didn't vacation; there was not enough time or finances. So having him out of town for any reason was unique. What was more unusual happened upon his return: He had brought me back a surprise.

As he handed over the small package, I thought I had never seen anything so beautiful. The wrapping was fancy, very fancy, with smooth, silvery paper and a huge, glistening bow. Along the ribbon was one of those stickers embossed with the name of the department store. Dad explained to me what a grand place it was.

Unless you have grown up in a home with precious few extras, you may not be able to appreciate fully what it means to receive something special like this. I stood there for many minutes just holding the precious gift in my hands, barely able to take it in.

Daddy smiled at me. "Go ahead, open it."

Carefully trying not to tear even the paper, I gingerly uncovered the small box and lifted the lid. Underneath, carefully folded tissue protected its contents.

As I pulled back the paper, I saw the most utterly beautiful thing I had ever seen: a small, white, seed pearl evening bag, with a delicate little handle also covered in hand-stitched pearls. Inside, glossy white satin lining contained a tiny pocket for holding a cosmetic item or compact. There was also a small label carefully embroidered with the store's name.

I stood there just holding the evening bag in my hands. Even today, I can remember exactly how my heart jumped. The pearls slightly rolled under my touch. I felt the soft fabric and imagined placing a pretty powder puff inside. I envisioned going to a dance someday, with a beautiful dress and carrying my little pearl evening bag.

Of course, from a certain vantage point, it was a completely nonsensical gift. It was over-the-top. I don't even know how Daddy afforded such a gift—and it was of no practical use either, which my mother quietly pointed out to him later. I was too young, too gangly, too far away from ever being invited to go anywhere by anybody.

But it didn't matter. The gift had already made its impression. This small pearl evening bag touched me somewhere deep inside. Here was the most important man in my life up to that point, my dad, saying to me, "One day you will be able to use this. You will be feminine and lovely and have a pretty dress and go to a wonderful ball. You will dance and enjoy life, and someone will love you someday as I do now."

This gift represented the essence of extravagance. Impractical, immoderate, lavish beyond measure. And truth be told, looking back, it was not the little pearl-covered evening bag itself, gorgeous as it was, that mesmerized me but rather how special it made me feel. My dad had looked past all the reality of where I was—a completely awkward teenager—to the time I would be a young woman. It filled me with a sense of wonder and excitement and hope. I'll never forget my little pearl evening bag.

God's love for us is like that: extravagant beyond words. It is lavish to the point of being nonsensical. It is unrestrained and exorbitant. It has no boundaries, nor can it be quantified. It comes to us while we are still awkward, stumbling, and lacking beauty. Yet, once we begin to perceive the sort of love He has for us—its utter immoderation and outrageous excessiveness—our innermost beings start to change. Because in the face of such unveiled extravagance, we catch a tiny glimpse of ourselves *as He sees us and what we could be*: beautiful, majestic, full of grace—pure and lovely as pearls on white satin.

But what are the actual characteristics of God's extravagant love toward us? Because what we call "extravagant" in this life often accompanies the greatest fragility. Must we alter our perceptions in order to understand such unrestrained bias on His part toward humankind? Is God extravagant with details? Does His extravagant love have an ending or run out? If His love is so exorbitant, why do we sometimes feel deprived?

In this study, we will examine characteristics of God's extravagant love for us. We will accomplish this through extensive research into the life and daily activities of ancient times. Here, buried within the cultural context of biblical history, we can discover amazing details which will help deepen our understanding of specific verses and passages in Scripture.

Like mining for diamonds, uncovering these historic jewels helps enrich our study of the Word of God. It will enlighten our knowledge of what was actually happening at the time an author penned a certain passage. Some of these details will be so surprising, I can hardly wait to share them with you. Then we will pull that history forward to lend a greater awareness of what these verses say to us today about God's passionate love toward mankind.

I am so glad you are going to embark on this journey with me. And I pray that this study will be as meaningful to you as a small pearl evening bag was to me many years ago.

CHAPTER 1

The Lesson of Simple Gestures

Extravagant Thoughtfulness: Mark 6:45

Extravagant, defined:
Merriam-Webster defines the word *extravagant* like this:

> extravagant (ik-stra-vi-gənt): *adj.* exceeding the limits of reason; extremely elaborate; lacking in restraint. Synonyms: profuse, lavish, bountiful.[1]

It carries the idea of something that is "over-the-top," as we would say.

What does the word *extravagant* mean to you? Think back. Have you ever known a person you would call extravagant? We mostly think of this attribute surfacing in a person's lifestyle, habits, and surroundings. And more often than not, extravagance involves possessions, a certain bent toward excess. In

Western culture, we associate extravagance with possessions, and by extension, wealth. It is connected with purchasing ability, and usually power.

So to link extravagance with a homeless person who had only one change of clothes and was an itinerant teacher dependent upon others for food and support seems a stretch. Yet Jesus was the most extravagant person who ever lived.

In order to even speak of Him in such terms, we have to think of extravagance in different ways, to redefine our notion of exorbitant, to cut new channels of thought in our minds and refocus our attention on inner attributes, spiritual aspects, the intangibles of relationship; to ponder anew what it means to be a caring person, a thoughtful person, and what defines humility. These lead us to ponder the fullness of God's love—extravagant beyond measure and exposed for all to see in the person of Jesus Christ.

Understanding that we can never wrap our minds around the vastness of His love for us, we will examine one facet of His love at a time. We will try to pull back the veil, so to speak, and peer into His extravagant love.

Love for the World, Love for One

Several months ago, I was listening to a minister quoting John 3:16. It's a verse that's probably the most familiar to believers and nonbelievers alike. So sometimes, when we hear it, we are almost *not* hearing it. Except on this occasion, there was something about the way the minister was emphasizing the words that caused me to get completely stuck on the very first phrase: "For God so loved the world . . ."

I began to think of the total, all-inclusive nature of that statement. It doesn't say He loves just believers and not those who don't love Him, or just one denomination and not another, but the world—totally, completely, with no qualifications whatsoever. Everyone, everywhere, regardless of who they are or the circumstances of their lives—He loves them.

Then, just recently, something occurred that started me thinking anew about the extravagant nature of God's love for us. It happened in a most unexpected way one Saturday morning when I often host "Prayer and Share" brunches in our home for women of all ages, normally with great turnouts.

On this particular Saturday, more than forty ladies had been planning to attend, but beginning on Friday night and continuing right through until the next morning, over half of those who had confirmed they were coming began canceling. They called, emailed, and texted, each one apologizing profusely about unexpected conflicts. Things come up. I totally realized that. However, I commented to my husband how odd it was, vaguely wondering if the Lord might be up to something.

Saturday morning dawned. My guests began arriving, including one beautiful young woman in her late twenties whom I had met only briefly. She had attended a few sessions of one of my Bible study classes at church, but other than that, I knew little about her. As the morning progressed, it became increasingly apparent that there was great need in her life.

For these brunches, I usually ask an older woman to share a little personal testimony. The younger women seem to love to hear these life experiences and journeys with the Lord. The woman I had asked on this particular day shared a deeply wounding experience she had gone through and God's faithfulness in leading her through it. Most of us—even those who had known her for a long time—had never heard her story.

As we moved into the part of our gathering where we each share prayer needs, the young woman happened to be seated where she was last to speak. When it came her turn, she began to cry. During the next half hour, she poured out her heart to us, explaining her extremely difficult circumstances and weeping all the while. To our surprise, many of her experiences closely paralleled those of the older woman who had shared her story with us that day. We surrounded the young woman, held her, prayed for her.

After everyone else left, my new friend stayed another couple of hours with me while I continued to minister and pray with her. My husband, normally at home on Saturday afternoons, had a previous engagement—an event unusual in and of itself which gave us one-on-one time. Finally, after she left my home, I had a quiet hour or so to pray and contemplate the day's events.

It occurred to me the entire Saturday morning may have been orchestrated by the Lord Himself to give this young person a safe place to open up—that the testimony of my older friend may have spoken to the younger woman in a very specific way; that perhaps, if a larger group had been present, it may have proved intimidating to speak as openly as the young woman felt free to do.

As I sat alone in the house praying for my new friend and all her challenges, I asked the Lord if, in fact, this was what He had had in mind. And in the stillness, I sensed Him saying to me, not as a rebuke but with piercing intensity nonetheless, "You do not understand how extravagant My love is . . . even for just one."

This thought came to me so plainly and so fiercely that I sat just thinking about it for a long time—the extravagance of His love for us, for *all of us*, men, women, and children all over the globe. Though flawed, stubborn creatures, humankind remains His grandest creation, and He cherishes us, desires only the best for us.

As I continued to meditate about the exorbitant nature of His love, I realized He also was revealing something else: numbers, per se, mean nothing to Him. He will go to the most incredible extremes to display His love to *one person*, as He so obviously did on that Saturday morning at my house.

We can be tyrannized by numbers. We measure success by numbers—how many attended, how many pledged, how many came forward to the front, how many were baptized.

And in point of fact, numbers do matter. We think of the earth's population, a staggering 7.9 billion, and the millions and millions of people who still haven't heard the name of Jesus. It can be overwhelming. We get frantic thinking of the numbers. And yet, let me quickly add, I do think we should be totally and completely aware of the vastness of these figures—after all, we have an entire book in our Bible called Numbers! And as we began, "For God so loved the world . . ."

Then something happens like that Saturday at my house. His immeasurable love, fully extended to the millions, suddenly focused with exquisite clarity on one individual . . . extravagance unveiled, even for just *one*.

They say confession is good for the soul. So here goes. I need this study as much as anyone. When you teach and write, it is so easy to get caught up in numbers. But God's love often can be witnessed orchestrating enormous events and circumstances in order to focus on one person—pulling back the veil, as it were, for one soul unknown by worldly standards and perhaps so suddenly and with such force of divine love as to be swallowed up by its brightness: *one heart* pierced by its laser-like precision . . . and yet for *all*. So we will begin and end our study in the only logical place we can: with the One who demonstrated love to *everyone* and to *every one*: Jesus Himself.

Jesus Lingers

Honestly? I had been a Christian many years before I ever heard anyone talking about a "life verse." In other words, a verse that somehow ministers to you in the very deepest recesses of your soul—a verse or passage you believe God Himself may have "given" you, so to speak, because you have such an incredibly close connection with the message whenever you read or think about it. You may already have a verse with this special sense of connection. And if you don't, you may want to ask God to give you one.

Here's how I first heard of "life verses." A visiting minister filled the pulpit one Sunday morning at my home church in Birmingham, Alabama. His name was Dr. Chuck Kelley, president emeritus of New Orleans Baptist Theological Seminary. That day, he began his sermon by telling us he intended to preach on his life verse, saying we would laugh when we heard what it was. And truly, it was a hilarious verse, something about a worm eating through the wood or some such, located in the Old Testament. I don't even remember exactly where.

Dr. Kelley explained that a life verse is one that seems to pierce your mind and heart, and does so each time you read it, maybe from the very first moment you come across it in Scripture. He said the verse literally jumps off the page as you read and think and pray about it. As he began to explain how God had always spoken to him through this particular verse every time he read it, we all understood the importance of the message to him.

It made me realize I also had a life verse but just hadn't recognized it as such. I remembered a little one-sentence verse which had had a profound effect on me the very first time I read it and continues to have the same effect even to this day. In fact, upon first reading it, I was so overcome with deep emotion, I laid my Bible down and wept.

Now, when I tell you what the verse is—this little one-sentence verse—I know what you are going to say to yourself. You are going to say, "That's not much of a verse," similar to our reaction to the verse Dr. Kelley shared with us in the congregation that morning.

But I think as we go through it word by word, you will catch a glimpse of the totality of Jesus's extravagant love for us, even down to very small matters of detail—in this case, a small gesture but under the circumstances, extraordinary. It will speak volumes about how He treated common, ordinary people in common, ordinary situations. We will see His exorbitant thoughtfulness for us.

The verse is Mark 6:45 from The Living Bible: "He Himself would stay and tell the crowds goodbye and get them started home." (See! I said you might scratch your head!)

Bits and pieces of this insightful little sentence have made it into all translations, but only in The Living Bible do we find the phrase collected together as one entire sentence. So how did I come across it, you're probably wondering?

Looking back, its hard to believe at the moment of my conversion at the age of thirty, I didn't own a single copy of Scripture—and this while writing numerous treatises, including a master's thesis in literature and working toward a doctorate in the same. Hundreds of books lined my home office but not a single Bible. What's more, I had never read a modern translation.

A few months after I became a Christian, a deep desire to read Scripture descended on me. I called my parents and asked them to send me a Bible. My dad told my mom to drop whatever she was doing and go to the bookstore.

Now here is where the story becomes amusing. Until the day she died, Mom maintained there was only one Bible in the entire bookstore—only one: a small, green leather volume of The Living Bible.

A few years later, I learned this particular rendering of Scripture was done by a man for his six-year-old son so the boy could understand easily what was being said. I had a good laugh to myself, guessing the Lord judged me to be about six years old at the time I received my Bible!

At first, all I wanted to do was read the four gospels—Matthew, Mark, Luke, and John—and then just what Jesus said. Shortly after receiving my Bible, I came across this one verse, in fact one sentence, that absolutely jumped off the page and into my heart. It pierced me completely, and I wept and wept. This continued for years afterward just thinking on it.

During this time in my journey as a believer, I didn't write or underline in my Bible. I had come to have such a respect for it and to treasure it so much, I didn't feel doing so would honor the beautiful life-giving words. (Now I mark up my Bibles to the extent that I have to purchase a new one each time I write a new study!)

But this verse made such an impact on me that I grabbed a yellow highlighter and underlined it. Let's take a look at it word by word.

Between Two Great Miracles

The tiny verse goes unnoticed mostly because it is sandwiched between two of the greatest events recorded in the New Testament: the feeding of the five thousand and Jesus walking on the water. But this one sentence yields enormous insight into what Jesus was really like, what His everyday demeanor was apart from performing miracles. Though perfectly capable of grand supernatural events, like supplying several thousand men, women, and children with supper and ruling over nature by ambling upright over fierce waves, Jesus Himself pulls back the veil to reveal to us His extravagant thoughtfulness in little gestures such as these.

Let's become a fly on the wall and study this scene. No doubt by now in His ministry, His reputation preceded Him. After all, if you lived somewhere in Galilee and heard about someone whose touch could heal any sickness, whose words soothed away all cares, who accepted everybody no matter how poor or wretched, you would find a way to hear and see him no matter what, if only out of curiosity. In today's parlance, he would have had rock star status. That's really what it must have been like.

This reminds me of a few years ago when my son, daughter-in-law, and their children were visiting us in Orlando from out of town. One afternoon, we all went to Downtown Disney, shopping in one of the larger stores there.

Suddenly, crowds of people began sweeping into the store, everybody talking at once, pushing, shoving, cameras clicking. We turned and caught a glimpse of what all the excitement was about: Michael Jackson had entered the store with a small entourage plus two of his children!

Complete pandemonium erupted. People were vaulting over countertops, even passing infants by hand, head over head, to complete strangers in hopes of getting a picture of Jackson holding their child. I really had never seen anything like it. And in light of full disclosure, when he walked by me, I asked his bodyguard if he would take my picture with him, and there you have it—I was photographed with Michael Jackson!

But I suspect, human nature being what it is, that crowds and crowds of people swept in to be close to Jesus for a hundred different reasons—many selfishly motivated, I'm sure. They pushed and shoved just trying to touch Him or His garments. Several times, the disciples complained they did not even have time to eat.

This sort of pressure and schedule, not to mention the hours of teaching and interaction with all sorts of personalities, had to have been exhausting. More than likely, Jesus's back got tired and His feet ached. And in fact, in Mark 6:31, He says to His disciples, "Come away by yourselves to a desolate place and rest awhile."

So He and the disciples climbed into a boat along the edge of the Sea of Galilee and began rowing to a more secluded location. But the crowds spotted Him from the shore and began to run along the water's edge to intercept Him when He finally landed.

By the time the disciples got back to shore with Him, the crowd had swelled to over five thousand. When He saw them, here is His reaction: "He had compassion for them, because they were harassed and helpless, like sheep without a shepherd" (Matthew 9:36).

History of the Sea of Galilee

There's nothing that helps an historic scene come alive like knowing something of the place and setting. So let's pause here a moment to visualize where Jesus was during this event and what the surrounding area looked like. For that, we turn our attention to the Sea of Galilee and travel back in time.

In the Bible, Scripture calls this large, freshwater lake by four names:

1. Sea of Galilee
2. Sea of Chinnereth (also Kinneret in Hebrew, meaning "harp-shaped")
3. Lake of Gennesaret
4. Sea of Tiberius

It is thirteen miles long and eight miles across at its widest point. The Jordan River flows into its northern tip, and several springs on its floor bubble up clean, fresh water continuously. Fish were abundant then, as they are today.

In first-century Israel, many towns and villages ranging in size dotted the shores of the lake. Archaeologists estimate the population of Capernaum, where Jesus lived and began His ministry, to be fifteen hundred to two thousand people, with substantial docking facilities and a thriving fishing industry.[2]

Other smaller villages stretched along the shoreline, with the main concentration of people around the northern regions of the lake. If you needed to get food, you stayed close to a place where fishing boats would come in. Generally in these little markets, someone would be selling fresh bread, perhaps fruit, and a few other food items. But once you began traveling southward around the lake's edge, there were some very isolated places. These areas were beautiful, but barren.[3]

It was around the lake's perimeter, going toward more desolate places, that Jesus and the disciples traveled by boat on this occasion. They were seeking a place "far from the madding crowd" in order to rest, but the people would not be denied. They could see Him from the shoreline, and they began to sprint, anticipating where the boat might be coming ashore. It was frenzied pushing and shoving, running and yelling.

Finally, I suspect Jesus said to the disciples something to the effect of, "Go ahead. Let's put to shore." Though presumably tired through and through, He sees people, desperate people, probably many of whom were beaten down by life. Understanding their plight, He is drawn to shore.

Now He begins to teach them, and they settle down in order to listen to what He is saying. Later, after much teaching (many scholars think this is where He delivered the great Sermon on the Mount), the disciples come to Him, and you can hear the urgency in their words.

"Master," one of them says, "send the crowds away so they can go to the surrounding villages and get something to eat—for the hour is late and we are in a desolate place."

At this moment, He tells the disciples they should feed the people. We know their infamous reply, "How in the world are we supposed to do that?" (We can almost hear the dismay in their voices!)

And of course, we know what happens. Jesus takes a young boy's five loaves of bread and two fishes, and the entire five thousand-plus people eat with baskets full of leftovers!

So it's a long day filled with lots of scrambling, snatching, shouting, and shoving. The disciples are charged with organizing and tending to the needs of five thousand people—demands everywhere.

Now comes our verse. At the end of this totally exhausting albeit wonderful event, Jesus dismisses the disciples. He tells them they can "call it a day," so to speak, but He Himself stays for a most extraordinary reason. He purposefully lingers to tell the crowds goodbye and to get them started home. It is a simple gesture full of love.

Here is where I like to use my imagination recreating this scene. Knowing human nature as we do, I'm sure the disciples simply said, "You got it, Lord—we can't get away from this place fast enough and just chill out." So they left . . . but not Jesus.

I can just see our Lord going from one group to another, perhaps reaching His hand down to help pull someone to their feet. Gathering what might remain of leftovers for them; lifting a child up from playing to place him safely in the arms of a parent; giving an elderly person a much-needed hug; placing a comforting hand on the shoulders of a poor father. With each touch, with each word, He hands over a little gift of extravagant thoughtfulness, so tender and so personal.

After being fed to overflowing, after seeing people healed, after hearing beautiful words of hope and comfort, probably not one single person would have thought less of Him had He left these closing moments to His disciples, or if all of them—disciples and Jesus—had just departed from them.

But that was not His nature. And I am certain that each and every one of those five thousand who were in attendance that day felt His final kind touch and heard His sweet goodbyes. If they turned around to catch one last glimpse of Him, I am certain they saw Him one more time—and I am certain He stood on that "desolate spot" at that "late hour" until each and every person was safely on their way home.

Lessons for Us Today

Let's look at this sentence one more time and soak in its wonderful message word by word.

The verse begins "He Himself . . ." So we begin here—Jesus will never ask us to do something that He Himself is not willing to do.

We each have times in our lives when we wonder if God understands what we are experiencing. Does He really understand our loneliness, our heartache, our disappointments? The answer is yes. He will not ask us to respond in a way "He Himself" is not willing to respond.

He could have left the crowds that day—no one would have thought less of Him, especially having just enjoyed a wonderful meal that cost them nothing. But He Himself stayed behind to add one last finishing touch, exhausted as He must have been: to leave no stone unturned, to personally bid them a safe journey home.

Remember where this entire scene is located. The Bible calls it a "desolate place." The disciples understood the gravity of their situation. They say to Him, "Lord, this is a desolate place and the hour is late." Whenever we find ourselves in a "desolate place," Jesus Himself remains with us. He does not leave us alone in our desolation. He stays with us, even—we can say especially—when the hour is late.

My friend, have you ever found yourself in a desolate place somewhere along your life's journey and, to make matters worse, the hour is late?

Jesus can turn a desolate place into a venue of abundance by His very presence. He can transform a late hour in your life into a moment of perfect timing. As He says, "I will never leave you or forsake you." And here, we clearly see a working out of this promise in His handling of their situation. He stays with us in our desolate places until we are safely on our way again.

The verse continues: "He Himself would stay and tell the crowds goodbye." Why did this bring me such great comfort when I first read these words? Because I immediately thought about Jesus telling His disciples that unless He went away (John 16:7), the Holy Spirit could not come to them.

At the time, they didn't fully realize the importance of what He was saying. But later, after Pentecost, they understood. Jesus was not leaving them at all, but coming to them in the form of the indwelling Spirit.

Our next point leads us to examine where Jesus was sending the crowd to—He was getting "them started home." When Jesus comes into our lives, He has one overriding purpose that rises above all others: He comes to us in order to start us on our journey "home."

And that home is our eternal biding place with Him and our Father, where we will live forever enjoying His company and our Father's. When Jesus comes into our lives, He gets us started home.

One of the most precious moments of my life came as I sat with my mother during her last few days on Earth. As some of you may know from my other Bible studies, mother and I were often at complete odds when I was growing up. In fact, we had a contentious relationship most of my life.

She was suffering from Alzheimer's, so I cared for her until she required a nursing home. Then I went every day to feed her. Along the way, she and I became close. She expressed love to me in ways she had never done before. As she grew weaker and less responsive, one of her attendants said the end was very near, estimating only another twenty-four to forty-eight hours.

I came early to her bedside and left late in the evening. Mother was completely unresponsive, so I just sat on her bed and thought perhaps, if she could hear me at all, she would enjoy listening to some of the old hymns she had enjoyed for years in church.

So I began to sing some of her favorites, songs such as "In the Garden" and "What a Friend We Have in Jesus." As I sang, I noticed she began to try to lift her hands straight upward. Her eyes were closed and her arms were so weak, but she tried to keep them lifted.

I couldn't figure out what in the world she was doing. My mother came from a very conservative church tradition. Very quiet, very still, very formal worship—she would never have raised her hands in praise as so many do today.

But when I would stop singing, her hands would go down. And when I would start back, her hands would go up. I couldn't come to any conclusion other than she was raising her hands in praise.

In fact, sometimes I placed my hands under her elbows to help her, because she seemed so intent on doing this.

At one point, though her eyes remained closed, as I was singing the part of "The Old Rugged Cross" where it says "and [we'll] exchange it [the cross] one day for a crown," I distinctly saw mother smile and under her breath utter a long "Uh-huh," the positive sound of affirmation. A minister friend of mine commented there is no telling what she was seeing during those moments. Mother passed away a few hours later. Jesus Himself had stayed with her in a desolate place and was seeing her home.

Wrapping Up

There remains today something so very poignant for me as I think about the scene that day by the shores of Galilee. Jesus had to have been tired, worn out probably. But He stayed. And if He would do that then for all those hapless, wandering souls, why would we ever think He wouldn't stay with us now . . . to the very end?

In some ways, I am more deeply moved by the awareness of this profound thoughtfulness in His nature than I am by the huge miracle of feeding all those people. It comforts me in more ways than the knowledge of His ability to walk on water ever will. He lingered with them as long as they needed Him; He touched them and held their hands; He helped them pick up their bundles; He spoke gentle words to them; He left none of this to anyone else—He attended to them Himself.

And I am certain He stood in that desolate place, watching *all* of them walk until the last *one* climbed over the last hill and arrived safely home.

Capernaum and the Sea of Galilee

Jesus chose the town of Capernaum to live when He began His ministry. During our Master's day, it probably boasted a population of around fifteen hundred to two thousand people, but because it was an important crossroads for travelers and marketers, many visitors passed through its gates each year. Located on the Sea of Galilee, it offered a small but substantial harbor with docks and piers for fishing boats and other lake traffic.[4]

Josephus, considered by many to be the best contemporary historian during Roman times, wrote this of Capernaum and the surrounding area:

The country also that lies over against this lake hath the same name of Gennesaret; its nature is wonderful as well as its beauty; its soil is so fruitful that all sorts of trees can grow upon it, and the inhabitants accordingly plant all sorts of trees there; for the temper of the air is so well mixed, that it agrees very well with those several sorts, particularly walnuts, which require the coldest air, flourish there in vast plenty; there are palm trees also, which grow best in hot air; fig trees also and olives grow near them, which yet require an air that is more temperate. One may call this place the ambition of nature, where it forces those plants that are naturally enemies to one another to agree together; it is a happy contention of the seasons.[5]

Questions for Discussion

1. If you have a "life verse" as described in Chapter 1, think about it now. What strikes you about the words, and what is meaningful in its message to you? If you do not have a "life verse," ask God to reveal one to you.
2. Sometimes a person might say he/she loves us, but they may not be particularly thoughtful. Do you know a person you would describe as thoughtful? What do you think makes him or her that way?
3. Explain a time or circumstance in your life when you think God exhibited thoughtfulness to you personally. This is not referring to a dramatic or even perhaps a miraculous event, but rather something He did for you that you would describe as a tender touch.

Closing Thoughts

God's love for us is accompanied by thoughtfulness for who we are as individuals—He knows our deepest needs and desires and what's best for each of us. We are always on His mind.

CHAPTER 2

The Lesson of the Almond Tree

Extravagant Commitment: Jeremiah 1:11–12

Our family cherishes a sweet personal connection with almonds. My husband's grandfather, born in 1868, carried the name Almond Horner. During his teen years, Mr. Horner dropped the *d* and simply spelled his name "Almon" for convenience's sake, but he enjoyed these delicious treats all his life.

The Scripture passage we will examine here pivots around a beautiful image of an almond branch—framed by a question, then a promise. It is found in the Old Testament with one of God's most favored servants, Jeremiah, near the start of the young man's journey as a prophet in approximately 626 BC.

Through the encounter, God provides him assurance of extravagant watchfulness over His Word. However, it is watchfulness accompanied by Jeremiah's commitment to make sure His Word is executed faithfully.

No matter how extravagant verbal expressions of love may be, they wear thin without deeds. Well-known author Toni Morrison speaks through one of her characters in vernacular language that either "love is or it ain't."[1] Thin love equates to no love at all.

Love reveals its depth through actions. When the authority of God backs up His commitment to see His Word accomplished, we can be confident each of His loving promises toward us will be carried out.

History of the Almond Tree

Let's take a moment to familiarize ourselves with a little history and some characteristics of this ancient tree. You may be surprised to learn just how long peoples all over the world have enjoyed its beauty and fruit.

Though the almond tree's exact ancestry remains a mystery—some believe it originated in China—the Mediterranean region's arid summers and mild winters perfectly suit the almond tree, to the extent it is now considered native in this part of the world. In ancient times, these fruit trees flourished all over the Levant, and once explorers began traveling early Silk Road routes, the tasty nut complemented meals throughout the region.[2]

Early Middle Eastern cultures added the nuts to flatbreads and sauces or ground them to a powder to include in various dishes. Ancient Egyptian chefs developed savory baked goods spiced with almonds, and archaeologists continue to find evidence of their use—including in King Tut's tomb, where a pot of almonds accompanied his other afterlife possessions. Often, almonds were enjoyed as they are today, straight from the tree.[3]

It seems appropriate that so wonderful a treat should be born from specimens of great loveliness. Through the centuries, almond trees' delicate, flowering branches have inspired artists to include the white-and-pink blossoms in paintings, sculptures, and *objets d'art*. Vincent van Gogh, so taken with their beauty, filled an entire canvas with nothing but their lacy blooms on a field of blue—a painting familiar to many through its wide use by publishers on journal covers, diaries, and stationery.[4]

Even today, the trees' blooms continue to enchant us. The well-known Italian design house of Dolce & Gabbana introduced its 2014 spring collection to praise within the haute couture world—a line of dresses, skirts, blouses, and sunglasses lavishly covered with almond blossoms, some sewn in 3D fashion. As sleek models paraded these scrumptiously patterned clothes down Milan runways, dozens of full-grown almond trees formed an ethereal backdrop across the platforms.[5]

The almond's tender five-petaled blossoms most closely resemble those of a peach or pear and can range in color from white with dark pink centers to gorgeous shades of pink. Trees grow to an average height of ten to fifteen feet, with a life span of twenty-five years. They begin bearing fruit about five years into growth.[6]

Today, California provides 100 percent of almonds produced for consumption in the United States and 70 to 80 percent of the world's supply.[7] Since almond trees require cross-pollination in order to bear fruit, the influx of beekeepers into the groves of the San Joaquin Valley from February through March[8] represents the largest "managed pollination event"[9] in the world.

Throughout history, many cultures have attached varying degrees of symbolism to the almond. One Greek legend claims a lovely bride-to-be named Phyllis wasted away of a broken heart as she waited in vain for her fiancé at the altar. As a way of showing their sympathy, the gods transformed her into an almond tree as a symbol of hope. When her fiancé returned, seeing only a leafless tree, he immediately embraced her, at which point the branches burst into blossoms. From this myth, there sprung up a general tradition of the almond tree representing hope.

As early as these accounts are, none predate the earliest biblical notations. So let's turn our attention to Scripture references to discover what they reveal to us.

Biblical References

Though the almond tree is referenced specifically only half a dozen times in Scripture, two of them do so in a way that shows it to be at the forefront of Jewish thought.

Genesis 43:11 depicts Joseph's brothers returning from Egypt. As they report to their father, Jacob, about a prince who demanded information concerning their family before giving them supplies to get through the famine, the old patriarch instructs them to take gifts back to him as evidence of their goodwill. Among these superior items, we find the subject of our lesson: "Then their father, Israel, said to them, 'If it must be so, then do this: take some of the choice fruits of the land in your bags and carry a present down to the man, a little balm and a little honey, gum, myrrh, pistachio nuts, and *almonds*.'" So we see that possibly as early as 2000–1800 BC (or earlier), people in the Levant considered almonds a *prized* food item.

Our next two encounters with almonds in Scripture however form the basis of an important image which resonates throughout the Bible. God Himself chooses the visual by singling out lovely almond blossoms as a key design component in Tabernacle and Temple furnishings. Then He goes a step further to ensure its symbolic significance in selecting Israel's priestly leaders. Both incidents take place during formative Wilderness years, as the Lord begins instituting elements of worship and service for the nation of Israel.

In Exodus 25–27, God gives Moses precise instructions for building His Tabernacle and all its furnishings. Working from these plans, artisans led by Bezalel and Oholiab crafted, among other pieces, a lampstand to furnish light inside the Holy Place. Receptacles holding oil and wicks atop the lampstand replicated the shape of five-petaled almond blossoms, a flower form perfectly suited to create a small cup. Then the lampstand and its branches were sculpted in similar fashion to resemble branches of the tree itself.

Hammered out of solid 22-carat (or higher) gold, the magnificent lampstand glowed with its own luster under flickering flames rising above seven blossom cups—one center cup with three on each side. Pure, beaten olive oil filled each cup containing a wick. Flames used for lighting this important piece came directly from the Altar of Sacrifice, which in turn had been lit by the Lord Himself—hence it was all holy fire.

Only one lampstand illuminated the interior of the Tabernacle. In the Temple, however, Solomon made ten lampstands designed just like that one and placed five down each side of a larger but similar room, also known as the Holy Place (1 Kings 7:49; 2 Chronicles 4:7). (You may recall the Holy of Holies shone only with the *shekinah* [glory] of God.)

The lampstand becomes a major symbol of God's light in the world, and the culmination of that light comes in the person of His Son, Jesus Christ. Jesus calls Himself the Light of the World and goes on to tell believers they also are the light of the world. All of this wonderful symbolism begins here, with a beautiful visual image from God's creation: a blossom from the lovely almond tree.

Next, in Numbers 17, we witness an incident when God's Chosen People question Moses's authority and Aaron's leadership. As Moses announces Aaron will serve in the important capacity of heading up the royal priesthood, most Israelites question his choice, signaling an underlying disbelief in God's authority over them.

To settle the issue, God instructs each of the twelve tribes to procure a tree branch, then carve the name of the tribe into its wood. It's not completely clear whether each branch is from the same tree or not, but what is clear is that Aaron selects an almond branch. Moses then collects the branches and places all of them within the Tabernacle. The next morning, Aaron's almond branch has not only budded, but blossomed, borne fruit, and produced almonds—a sequence which normally takes seven to eight months. As a result of God's miraculous intervention, the almond branch becomes a symbol for divine authority.

In summary, we see a general tradition of symbolism attached to the almond tree representing hope, echoing in legends and Greek mythology. Then in Scripture, we note God utilizing an almond tree to underscore His dominion over events on Earth.

There remains one important last characteristic unique to almond trees, but I will save that until later in our discussion.

Hearing God's Voice

Now let's turn our focus to the verses themselves. Jeremiah 1:11–12 begins thus: "And the word of the Lord came to me, saying . . ." We meet the prophet himself recording one of his very first encounters with God. What makes his beginning statement noteworthy is Jeremiah immediately recognizes who is speaking to him. The start of any conversation we might have with the Lord begins here: We must be able to recognize His voice.

Earlier in Chapter 1, the Lord extends a "call" on the life of this young boy, the son of a priest, during the reign of Josiah (641–601 BC). We read at the outset God designated him to be a prophet as part of His plan, when he was still in his mother's womb. In fact, God goes on to claim Jeremiah was "consecrated" before he was even born.

Though we may not be called as prophets, Scripture assures us God knows our "frame" even when we are in our mother's womb. There is an extravagant sense of continuity in our lives once we fully comprehend what God is saying here. We live out our lives, not as mere accidents—there is divine purpose from the very moment of conception.

What we see here, however, may be something we also have experienced along the way. Jeremiah feels totally unqualified to answer the call from Yahweh, yet later he becomes one of Israel's greatest prophets. Sprinkled throughout the book, we find a recurring phrase, "And the word of the Lord came to me saying . . ." Jeremiah could recognize "the voice."

Can you do that? I ask the question because I think it's something we need to consider. We live at such breakneck speed today, hurriedly moving from one activity to another. Busyness defines us.

So here's the issue: How fast does God need to speak in order to match your schedule? Admittedly, Jeremiah lived during a time when life itself was much slower-paced, with far more time to just sit and contemplate and far fewer distractions of all the sort we know only too well. But there must be some amount of purposeful time set aside to give ourselves a great opportunity—the chance for the Word of the Lord to come to us.

When God Asks Questions

Have you ever wondered why Jesus asked so many questions? With some poor, blind person begging before Him, Jesus would ask, "What do you want me to do for you?" He walked along in a crowd with people pushing against Him on all sides and stopped to question, "Who touched me?" Other times, He asked, "Why do you call me good?" "Is it not written . . . ?" "What did Moses command you?" The list is endless. The Savior taught with as many questions as He did statements.

Jesus learned the technique from His Father. God asked questions of His prophets and His people, rulers and peasants alike, all throughout Old Testament events. It really began as early as the Garden of Eden when God asked Adam and Eve that reverberating question: "Where are you?"

Sometimes God answers His own questions. At first blush, He often appears to sum up a situation with statements totally at odds with the flow of conversation . . . occasionally at odds even with His own questions. But if we explore God's motives for using questions, it will lead us to an enlarged understanding of how He views things. So why did God ask so many questions throughout

Scripture—and more to the point, why does He continue to do that to us today?

First: He wants His hearers *to think*. Once a person activates his/her mind toward an issue, they begin to assess for themselves the subject at hand. Thinking about how to answer a question forces the process to begin.

God has blessed us with remarkable brains in order to contemplate events or explore circumstances. He openly wishes for us to use our mental abilities to the fullest extent possible as we grow in our knowledge of Him—not just to take someone else's opinion and adopt it for our own but to make what we believe a result of personal pursuit. When we "dig," Jesus becomes real to us . . . and our trust in Him solidifies.

Often, however, people spend enormous amounts of time thinking about everything *except* their faith. The well-known English Bible scholar John Stott, who co-edited *The Bible Speaks Today* series, says in his commentary on Romans that there are degrees of faith—our faith can be strong or weak. How then does it grow?

> Above all else through the use of our minds. Faith is not burying our heads in the sand, or screwing ourselves up to believe what we know is not true, or even whistling in the dark to keep our spirits up. On the contrary, faith is a reasoning trust. There can be no believing without thinking.[10]

Second: The questions reveal God's desire for us *to evaluate with Him*. When you think about that, at a certain level, it is remarkable He desires to do such a thing. But it is His way of draw-ing us into His sphere of thinking; He engages us to look at things with Him, to explore possibilities and ideas based on *His* way of evaluating. With questions, He leads us to consider what He wants us to consider.

Nowhere in the Bible is there more evidence for our premise than in Job 38–41. Through a plethora of questions, God demon-strates Job's lack of power and authority in the universe, compared to His total dominion. In the process, we glimpse His complete awareness of what transpires throughout creation, not just the gargantuan events but the minutest details. Scripture reminds us He knows when a mountain goat gives birth to her young; He observes what is happening in the ocean's depths.

Third: His entreaties to evaluate with Him *extend dignity to us.* God shows Himself to be far more than just Creator; He shows Himself to be a loving Father who cares deeply about His children. Because He made us in His image, we represent His most spec-tacular creation, and He respects our personhood.

Fourth: We come at last to His ultimate purpose: *To evaluate with Him provides an incredible opportunity for us to become acquainted with Him.* No one desires more than the Lord Himself for us to experience Him and to learn about Him accurately. And in order to leave nothing to chance, God assigns a special 24/7 tutor, the Holy Spirit, just for this undertaking.

God's Specific Question

So with acknowledgment of a purposeful attempt on our part to connect with God, we come to the interesting question He poses in our passage, one that is asked of us as well as the young prophet: "Jeremiah, what do you see?"

It's a simple question with profound implications. Essentially, God acts as an optician. He sets up an "eye" chart, just like when we go to get glasses. He wants to check Jeremiah's vision . . . and ours as well. No amount of studying about God enhances understanding of Him unless we are seeing as He sees.

Once again, Stott leads us to consider our Creator's viewpoint.

> God's complaint is that we do not really "seek" him at all, making his glory our supreme concern, that we have not set him before us, that there is no room for him in our thoughts, and that we do not love him with all our powers.[11]

Therefore, in order to achieve our goal of increased understanding about how our Creator thinks, we need to involve ourselves actively for the task. Let's consider three steps which will help our cause.

First: We must seek to see. Don't automatically assume you are seeking to see. Though we may be active in church and involved in Christian activities, we still may not be actively pursuing "seeker" status—we may actually be more interested in just being entertained, being involved with a group, or being social. These things are different from inwardly and actively "seeking."

Second: We must seek to see spiritually. Again, don't assume you are seeking spiritual things. We hear often of people before they become Christians describe their newness of "mind and heart" as an awakening. They feel like blinders have been removed. When I first became a Christian, this is exactly how I felt. Everything I had previously believed had to be reevaluated in light of my Savior, what He had done for me, and His hold on my life.

As the years rolled on, however, I began to realize what a process it really is. Because as we journey, we may need adjustments along the way; we may need to take time to refocus spiritually. We must be of a mindset to explore things with thoughtfulness toward our Creator's viewpoint.

Third: We must seek God's help to see clearly. Each of us can think of times when some situation existed in our lives which we could not understand at all. We prayed and asked God to do a certain something. Perhaps, however, we would do well to ask Him how He views the event or circumstance. Don't assume He evaluates an issue as you are evaluating it. Of course, He will never go against His stated Word in any way, but so often, we just don't have all the facts of a situation. We may think we do, but in reality, only God is in a position to know all there is to know of circumstances—and to know what's best for all involved.

Back to our verse and Jeremiah's conversation with the Lord. After God asks the young prophet, "What do you see?" Jeremiah answers he sees an almond branch. So before we continue further with our study of these verses, let's do a little additional exploration into the world of horticulture to ascertain why God might have chosen this specific tree during His encounter with Jeremiah.

God's Promise

I mentioned earlier I'd save one final characteristic of the almond tree until last. One unique ability distinguishes it from all other fruit trees: An almond specimen buds before any other fruit tree during the new year's season of growth. In fact, its flowers appear before its leaves appear.[12]

Farmers and growers know when the almond tree buds, spring will follow soon. And though it then takes eight months for the tree to go through its complete cycle of budding, blossoming, forming fruit, and ripening, the almond branch leads the way to bearing fruit.[13] One could say, it seeks early and eagerly to fulfill its purpose.

It is this matchless element God zeroes in upon when talking to Jeremiah. He likens it with His own commitment to His Word—really, an amazingly extravagant commitment to His Word. And in turn, this extravagant commitment exists for one specific reason: to see that His Word is performed without delay, quickly and completely.

Here is what the Lord says to Jeremiah once the young prophet correctly identifies the image: "I am watching over my Word to perform it" (Jeremiah 1:12). The Hebrew word for almond is *shaked* and actually means "hasten." According to Dr. H. B. Tristram in his *Natural History of the Bible*, the word borders on a poetical expression meaning "that which is awakening."[14]

However, when God says, "I watch over my Word," the word He uses for "watch over" is *shoked*. He makes a pun or play on words. What is before Jeremiah's eyes in the form of an almond branch becomes an object lesson of how God tends to His Word: He is diligent, He is committed, He watches over His Word with eagerness; He makes sure His Word is not just performed, but performed quickly, with all haste.

What a beautiful and comforting thought for us. God Himself, rather than being a disinterested bystander once words come from His mouth, actually continues to watch over precisely what He has said. Nothing will be left to chance, and nothing will ever be left undone.

When we hear His extravagant commitment, it may sound hollow, because our experiences with human beings often tell us something quite different. Think about your experiences. How often have you been disappointed with someone because they didn't do what they said they were going to do? We have all had moments such as these.

My husband has a friend who uses the following statement as the axiom on which he bases all his business dealings. In fact, he built a large corporation from the ground up using this as his number one priority. Each employee carries a card at all times printed with it:

> We must do exactly what we say we are going to do, exactly when we say we are going to do it, or contact the parties involved. This contact should be made prior to our appointment or promised delivery. This policy is important for all relationships, family, customers and fellow employees! It is mandatory for all employees and suppliers of H & H Products Co.

Along the way, most employees upheld the company's policies. What we possess in God, however, is a divine deity who has the ability to carry out all His Word, and He does so with eagerness. When God says something, He means it. He has the power and authority to back up what He says He's going to accomplish. He does exactly what He says He is going to do, and here we have a direct promise that He Himself watches over His Word. It is an extravagant statement, yet nonetheless a fact we can count on.

I don't know about you, but I find these verses incredibly comforting. It means we can expect with complete confidence the fulfillment of all God has proclaimed, because He Himself supervises His Word. He knows what He has said and what He has promised and what is recorded in the Bible, and He Himself supervises to see it is accomplished. Like the faithful almond tree, which eagerly reaches to fulfill what it was created to do—produce fruit early—God watches over His Word with extravagant attention, a promise of commitment we can rely upon.

In my studies, I've come to treasure and cling to these two short verses in the opening chapter of Jeremiah. I pray as we examine them together, you will find their message as encouraging as I do. And we can agree with C. S. Lewis, who once said the three most important words in all Scripture are these: "It is written . . ."[15]

Fast Facts about Almonds

1. Almonds, though often referred to as nuts, are actually the pit or seed from the tree's fruit, known as the drupe.[16]
2. The first reference to almonds in the Bible is as early as Genesis 43:11, when Jacob suggests sending almonds to Joseph in Egypt as a gift.
3. The tomb (c. 1325 BC) of Tutankhamen contained an abundant supply of almonds as part of his provision for the afterlife.[17]

4. Bees are required for cross-pollination, although growers currently are striving to discover and develop species which are self-pollinating.[18]

5. Wild almonds are bitter, whereas domesticated almonds are sweet. Eating just a few dozen wild almonds can prove fatal because they produce cyanide. How early man learned to distinguish between the two (in other words, choosing the one not lethal out of all the wild cultivars) remains a mystery.[19]

Questions for Discussion

1. List three things to which you are committed presently. What evidence could you present to demonstrate your commitment to each of these?

2. Have you ever broken a commitment to a relationship or some other particular thing to which you once were strongly committed? Think about the reasons. Do you regret the broken commitment now?

3. Can you think of a person to whom or situation in which you need to renew your commitment? What steps could be initiated to renew the commitment?

4. No matter how hard we try, there may be extenuating circumstances beyond our control that cause us to forego our commitments. Name some things beyond your control that might hinder you from keeping a commitment. For example, a change of financial

status or physical wellbeing might keep you from fulfilling a commitment, even though you wish to keep it.

Closing Thoughts

Ultimately, our fragility might affect our commitments, but not so with God. Once He makes a commitment, He keeps it—and there is nothing He is more committed to than His Word, the love letters from His heart.

CHAPTER 3

The Arts of Refining and Fulling

Extravagant Diligence: Malachi 3:2–3

As my family entered the exhibit room at the Florida Museum, it took a moment for our eyes to adjust to the darkness. A foyer of black walls and curtains heightened our anticipation for what awaited in the next room. But hardly anything could truly prepare us as we rounded the corner.

There, underneath the high-intensity, pinpoint lights, gleamed King Tutankhamun's coffin, covered in gold foil. The glow emanating from the curved and bejeweled face mask atop the coffin, also completely covered in gold foil, danced with a yellowy richness hard to describe. It was mesmerizing.

As I stood next to the stunning exhibit, I tried to imagine what a pharaoh might have looked like in the flesh, bedecked with gold and fine clothes—the best that ancient craftsmen could produce. Most of my family had moved on to the next room, but I continued to linger there beside the coffin, just staring at the glowing artifacts from thousands of years ago.

The gold jewelry held my gaze. I wondered what it would have been like to wear such a necklace. My mind drifted to what it might have been like to be dressed in a gown of soft, gauzy linen—the fabric of choice for royalty during the reign of Pharaohs.

It was a peek into another world, a world the writer of the last book in the Old Testament certainly knew about. The prophet Malachi uses several references to these remarkable crafts—imagery to highlight his key points. Our delving into the historic background will only enhance our understanding of two of the most well-known verses in the entire Old Testament and some of the very last utterances before the four-hundred-year veil of silence descends—before the birth of Messiah.

Gold and Linen

Gold and linen have two things in common: First, in their natural states, they are replete with impurities, and second, they require steadfast diligence to extract these impurities. Enter the refiner and the fuller, who practice two of the oldest crafts in the history of mankind, perhaps dating back as far as 2000 BC.

Unlike other professions whose products may conceal inherent flaws, refining and fulling produce easily discernible results. These results lay bare the diligence of the worker for all to see. The gold and linen accomplish nothing. They lay dumb and mute. It is only through sustained supervision of refiner and fuller that beauty and value surface within the ore and the cloth. The more diligent the craftsman, the more beautiful and valuable the final product becomes.

In the ancient book of Malachi, a prophetic passage often read at Christmastime refers to both professions (Malachi 3:2), leading us to consider what is involved in each. The fact that the Lord Himself is called a refiner and a fuller seals the importance of the analogy. Why? Because we are the gold and the linen, recipients of His steadfast handiwork to bring perfection upon our souls.

A Brief History of Refining

Scant written evidence continues to fuel speculation among mineralogists for dating earliest attempts at refining. Most historians accept 500 BC, but many claim 2000 BC or earlier as entirely possible. All agree, however, that ancient Egyptians were master goldsmiths, as the many exquisite artifacts recovered by archaeologists from tombs and other sites testify.[1]

What glimpses we have into early mining in Egypt derive from several sources, including written documentation. In the second century BC, a Greek geographer named Agatharchides of Cnidus traveled throughout Egypt recording many societal activities, including gold mining methods.[2] Later, in 60 BC, another historian, Diodorus Siculus, also traveled widely in the same area, notating his own observations plus many of the earlier reports by Agatharchides.[3] Both men reveal the incredibly difficult conditions of mines where slaves, criminals, and men, women, and children captured in battle were forced to labor continuously to dredge up ore from beneath the earth.

Once the rock was raised to the surface, skilled workers ground the stone, then washed away lighter impurities. The heavier ore remained. Next, another group of skilled laborers took this ore, placed it in earthen jars with some kind of flux—salt, tin, or lead perhaps—and sealed the lids. These earthen crucibles were placed in ovens or stone furnaces or even large holes dug into the ground. Firing brought temperatures up to 800 degrees centigrade and was maintained for five days and nights.[4]

At the completion of the firing process, the jars were taken out and allowed to cool. Then their lids were removed; what remained was pure gold.[5]

Here is how Diodorus Siculus summed up his observations:

> At the end of this period [five successive days and nights], when they have let the jars cool off, of the other matter [flux] they find no remains in the jars, but the gold they recover in pure form, there being but little waste. This working of the gold, as it is carried on at the farthermost borders of Egypt, is effected through all the extensive labors here described; for Nature herself, in my opinion, makes it clear that whereas the production of gold is laborious, the guarding of it is difficult, the zest for it very great, and that its use is halfway between pleasure and pain.[6]

The steps described above basically outline how gold is still refined today, of course with more advanced techniques and equipment. The purpose of the refiner, however, remains exactly the same: to render the purest possible gold, with little or no impurities.

Gaius Plinius Secundus, known as Pliny the Elder, made these observations in his *Natural History*, produced in AD 77 while living in Rome:

Gold is the only thing that loses no substance by the action of fire. As a matter of fact, it improves in quality the more often it is fired, and fire serves as a test of its goodness. Moreover in steady resistance to the overpowering effect of the juices of salt and vinegar it surpasses all things, and over and above that it can be spun into thread and woven into a fabric like wool.[7]

In gold refining, the term "testing" actually refers to what the refiner sees with his own eyes. Unlike other metals that might require demonstrating in some way its strength or subjection to additional measures to determine its purity, gold testing largely rests on what the refiner observes as he submits the gold to its fiery process.[8]

My husband has helped me immensely in understanding the process. As a dentist, he has melted down gold for crown and bridge preparation numerous times. Today, of course, mostly porcelain is utilized for these procedures, but not too long ago, gold was used almost entirely.

In his laboratory, he would place the mineral in a small, crucible-type cup and submit it to intense heat from a handheld torch. As any impurities present are burned away and the gold begins to become liquid, my husband says there comes a moment when the gold suddenly shines so brightly as to almost quiver, like it's alive. Before he brought it to my attention, I had never really noticed the difference between fourteen- and eighteen-carat gold. But when you look carefully, you see they are not the same. Eighteen-carat is much richer, more golden in color. When you jump to twenty-two- or twenty-four-carat, the gold glows with a depth, almost a fieriness that is simply beautiful to look at. It becomes so reflective you can see yourself in it.

There is an incredible scene in the movie *The Hobbit: The Desolation of Smaug* when the heroes melt enormous amounts of gold in huge furnaces. When it liquefies, it shines as if lit. The sight of that much gold flowing through dozens of metal funnels lights up the dark underground caverns where the scene takes place. The glowing gold is mesmerizing.[9]

We can envision a seasoned refiner seated at his work, carefully firing each chunk of ore to bring about the purest possible gold. His work requires intense concentration and an eye keen for its task. But beneath his competent hands, gold's glory emerges.

A Brief History of Fulling

Now let's turn our attention to fulling, a lesser-known craft than refining but with similar goals and expectations. In this case, however, instead of fire, the fuller relies on sun, water, and bleach to accomplish his work. Again, we can look for historical evidence of this venerable profession from ancient Egyptians, ranked among the greatest producers of fine linen the world has ever known.

During the long history of textile production, many fabrics have duplicated the quality of this linen. Over the years, I have had the good fortune to sew with some very fine materials. But while some fabrics may have duplicated the quality of these linens, few, if any, have surpassed them. We are talking about arguably the finest fabric ever produced by human hands.

The history of linen production in the ancient world is fascinating. Linen is made from flax, a plant with small leaves, blue flowers, and stems about four feet tall.[10] Flax grew abundantly along the Nile, an area where climate and moisture provide ideal growing conditions. When harvested, the flax was not cut but rather pulled out of the ground—backbreaking work done mostly by men. Half-pipe, young stems were the best. The fibers were then soaked, beaten, stripped, spun, twisted, and woven on a loom.[11]

According to experts on ancient textiles, it required about one year and at least sixteen steps to produce clothes from flax plants.[12] The resulting fabric is one of incredible beauty and fineness: extremely supple yet extremely strong.

In its natural state, however, linen is brown and dirty-looking, full of nubby imperfections. To create white linen, the cloth was washed in the Nile River or in canals, rinsed, pounded with stones, and bleached in the sun over and over again to get it white.[13] But it took weeks, perhaps even months, to get it that way. The diligence and skill of the fuller, a person who whitened fabric, determined the results. The best fuller was the most zealous fuller, diligent in his work.

From a workplace usually located near an ample water supply, the fuller would subject the linen fabric to a regimen of washing, scrubbing, pounding, and drying in the sun over and over until the desired color materialized. Usually, some abrasive soap or bleach product may have been part of the process.[14] (In Roman times, human urine was utilized because of its ammonia content. Subsequently, it became such a sought-after commodity that the government levied taxes on urine itself!)[15]

Several Bible passages refer to the Fuller's Field (2 Kings 18:15–17, Isaiah 7:1–3, Isaiah 36:1–2), generally thought to be located somewhere near the Gihon Springs of Jerusalem, which provided enough flowing water for fullers in that locale to complete their work of removing all debris and all impurities from the cloth. A fuller also required a minimum of twenty acres in order to spread out the linen to dry and bleach under the sun.

Our Lord: Refiner and Fuller

In our beautiful passage from Malachi, in verses with which you are likely familiar, the prophet speaks of the coming day of the Lord: "But who can endure the day of His coming, and who can stand when He appears? For He is like a refiner's fire and like fullers' soap" (Malachi 3:2).

Subsequently, in a New Testament passage, Peter, James, and John accompany Jesus up on a high mountain. Mark writes that Jesus's garments become radiant, "intensely white, as no one on earth could bleach them" (Mark 9:3). The two crafts, refining and fulling, were highly developed in biblical times.

Knowing that our Lord works as refiner and fuller, let's think about what impact His exorbitant diligence will have on us. We will begin by studying five characteristics of these ancient crafts.

First: Refiners and fullers strive toward perfection in their finished products, both in gold and in linen. It is a measured and patient work, where diligence produces the best results. Charles Spurgeon, the great nineteenth-century minister, calls this the "pace of perfection," a wonderful term that reminds us how "process-oriented" is our own journey toward spiritual maturity.[16]

Second: Refiners and fullers work toward exposing the beauty within the gold and linen. The fire and washing help give both materials perceivable beauty—it is present all the time, but it is the labor of the refiner and fuller that brings it to the surface.

Third: Refiners and fullers strive toward purifying the gold and linen. Removing foreign debris, dirt, and other substances requires constant checking and resubmitting the gold and linen to the process of cleansing. The gold is meant to be pure gold; the linen is meant to be fine linen. The purifying process is meant to bring each to its highest and best state.

Fourth: Refiners and fullers do not seek to alter the *essential* essence of the gold or the linen, but rather to eliminate anything not perfect, not *belonging* to the essential nature of purest gold or finest linen.

Fifth: Refiners and fullers work until they achieve their goal. It may require refiring, rebleaching, or additional washing, but until the gold gleams and the linen shines with whiteness, they will not cease.

Lessons for Us Today

The arts of the refiner and fuller were skills of great antiquity. Both lengthy and laborious processes, the desired results did not occur quickly. Much depended on the skill level and expertise of the craftsmen. We are like gold and linen. In our natural state, we are filled with extraneous material, debris, and imperfections.

What poignant symbolism for us today! As we relinquish more and more of our hearts and minds to the Lord, He cleanses us, purifies us, and washes us—to render us whiter, cleaner, purer, and more like His Son every day. We can willingly comply with this process, or we can resist. I think sometimes we don't even realize we are resisting. We just don't perceive certain places within our own personalities that are in need of cleansing, like blind spots: others may see them, but we don't. The first and best place to begin is by asking the Lord to reveal where these blind spots are—you may be surprised what He reveals to you.

From the same sermon by Charles Spurgeon referenced above, I came across this quote, appropriate for our study on God's extravagant love:

> Perfect love seeks the perfection of the thing it loves. Such is the perfect love of Christ—whenever He comes to a soul in love He comes as a refiner. He comes with this objective—to take away the dross from the silver and to make the fine gold purer still. In His sharpest dispensations He means no ill to us, but the divinest good, seeking not to grieve, but to lead us to the eternal blessedness, of which the root and flower are both found in absolute perfection. If any of you, my Hearers, are seeking the Lord at this time, I want you to understand what it means—you are seeking a fire which will test you and consume much which has been dear to you.[17]

Examine that last phrase just for a moment. I suspect Spurgeon had in mind that often those things God would seek to remove from our personalities, minds, and hearts are things within ourselves we have grown quite fond of, things God Himself may find far less attractive. God doesn't rest when we come to Him. His work in us continues on, and He has one goal before Him: to mold us as closely as possible to the likeness of His Son, Jesus. I think we sometimes say this without really examining what it means.

Flux and Bleach

What methods does God use to draw out our imperfections, or as the New Testament would say, to "sanctify" us? Let's look at four of the predominant means, our Lord's flux and bleach.

First: God uses our relationship with His Son, who is the standard against which all men and women will someday be judged. Our images are being transformed gradually into the image of Jesus, our elder brother. His likeness forms the family likeness. Second Corinthians teaches that "we all with unveiled face, beholding the glory of the Lord, are being transformed into the same image from one degree of glory to another. For this comes from the Lord who is Spirit" (2 Corinthians 3:18).

As we contemplate our Lord's time on earth, His example of treating people and attending to their needs, we have a clear concept of what our lives should look like. As God works to refine our souls, we do not have to wonder where He is taking us; He is forming us into the likeness of His Son.

Second: God uses His Word to teach, cleanse, and purify. A few years ago, the senior pastor of our church challenged all of us to begin each New Year by asking for a "word" from the Lord that would be our word for that year.

The first year, I prayed and felt the Lord was leading me toward the word "cleansing." I was pleased with my word. I thought it would be a good exercise for me to spend a year meditating on cleansing and what it meant in my life. After all, I had been a

Christian for many years at that point, and I felt it was probably time for a good "cleaning," so to speak.

The only problem came the second year when I prayed again for a new word to begin the cycle. I prayed with relish, wondering which word I would receive this time. Over and again, I sensed a certain word and would go back to the Lord with something to the effect of, "Are you sure, Lord?" But without a doubt, my word the second year was "purifying."

Candidly, I began to worry just a bit. But I launched into a second year of meditating on the subject of purifying.

I've got to admit, I came to the end of that second year and the beginning of the third year with a little trepidation. Would God again give me a year of praying and studying about cleansing and purifying?

As I began to pray, a quiet, still voice spoke into my heart at the beginning of the new year. My new word was "holiness"—not mine but His. And I realized what was happening. God had led me through two years of contemplating the necessity of my own cleansing and purifying in order to get me ready to even approach reflecting upon His holiness.

Scripture never leaves us unaffected. We either respond to it in positive ways or we turn against it. But for a believer, there can never be a neutral response.

Third: God uses the circumstances of our lives to teach, to cleanse, and to purify. I've heard many people admit they learn more from the challenges in their lives than they do from the easy times. I know that has been true in my own life. Difficulties drive us to dig in, looking to the One in whom we gain strength and put our hope.

But wonderful circumstances can teach also. We learn of God's generosity, His mercy, His extravagant love. These are the blessed times, and we rejoice when we realize that the day is coming when blessedness will fill all our moments as we live in His Presence forever.

Fourth: God uses relationships with others to refine us. Have you ever noticed that when a certain type of personality challenges you, it seems as if you no sooner finish dealing with that person, than another person with just the same sort of personality appears on the horizon? I've often wondered if that just isn't God's way of showing us how far we have to go in order to be as compassionate and merciful as His Son is to everyone—even those souls who frustrate us beyond belief!

Yet again, God can use relationships to purify and cleanse us, and it is a glorious experience. We meet other, more mature Christians who inspire us—who accept us and love on us—and it teaches us things in ways hard to express in words. Their examples then turn into real advances in our own efforts to "be more like Jesus."

Three Elements of Malachi 3:3

Let's look at three main elements within Malachi 3:3: the attitude of the refiner and fuller, the goal of the refiner and fuller, and the result of the refiner and fuller's work.

First: The verse indicates that the refiner "sits." At first blush, sitting might be mistaken as indifference. But knowing the meaning of the term used here suggests something quite different.

The word utilized here is the same used elsewhere in Scripture for the term meaning "sitting as a king sits on his throne."

Spurgeon makes note of this in a sermon he titled "The Sitting of the Refiner." The takeaway for us is that it indicates an attitude of complete control without any sense of rushing or hurry. When a king sits on his throne, he observes circumstances from a position of authority and power. His demeanor is relaxed and confident because everything is under his control. He knows what he is doing. This is the picture here. God leaves nothing to chance in our lives.

Second: The goal of our Lord as refiner and fuller is to rid us of all imperfections, to bring us into alignment with the nature of His Son. We touched on this previously. God works with us, not in a random fashion, but with a specific image in mind.

There is a thoroughness about it as well. He doesn't stop until He is satisfied. Just like the refiner and fuller of ancient times did not stop until they held pure gold in their hands or felt the beauty of washed linen, our Refiner and Fuller works to satisfy no one but Himself.

Third: God fires and washes toward a specific goal. Examine the last phrase in the verse—"and they will bring offerings in righteousness to the Lord." The result of our cleansing, the refining of our souls, culminates in the quality of our offerings to God: they are righteous, pure, and clean. These qualities in God's children bring glory to Him and His great Name. We are purified so that our gifts might be pure.

Mostly, I think we focus on what "gifts" come to us from the Lord. And Scripture does show that He gives and gives to His children. But our ultimate purpose in this lifetime—and, we might add, also in the next—is to bring gifts to the Lord, to lay at His feet what is His due.

We Are His Gold and Linen

Somehow all of this reminds me of an incredible moment I experienced when I was thirteen years old. My parents had enrolled me in classes with a piano teacher from our church who believed I showed some promise. This sweet lady finally announced one day she had taught me all she could and began urging my parents to allow me to audition before the leading pianist/teacher of Montgomery, Alabama, Miss Lillian Gill, who awarded a scholarship to one student each year.

Her reputation was widely known throughout the South. As a young woman, she had studied in Europe in a line of Franz Liszt pianists and then went on to have a remarkable career playing concert tours throughout the world—until a terrible automobile accident in Paris brought her back home to Montgomery, paralyzed from the waist down, confined to a wheelchair, and vowing never to play in public—or for that matter, in private—again.

After several years, she began to take on a few selected students, but by referred audition only. My piano teacher made all the arrangements, and on an early spring evening, I found myself headed toward a meeting that would have tremendous repercussions.

I'll never forget that first night I walked into Miss Gill's house on South Hull Avenue. She was from an old Southern family steeped in wealth and tradition, and lived in the family's home with her spinster sister. Filled with antiques, creaking wood floors muffled by Oriental rugs, and oil portraits hanging everywhere, most of the space in that enormous living room was taken up by two long, back-to-back concert Steinway grand pianos. There was utter silence as I walked into her world, except for a grandfather clock droning patiently away somewhere down a hallway.

Miss Gill sat in her wheelchair beside one of the pianos. After I introduced myself, she waved me on to the piano bench. I adjusted my sheet music and began to play. It was at this point that things took a sudden turn for the worse.

What I considered music "worth" playing consisted primarily of popular tunes. I believe I started off with some song by Elvis Presley, and I was really giving it my all. By the time I was headed into a little Jerry Lee Lewis, Miss Gill let go a "great ball of fire" of her own. She took her baton, slammed it down on the piano and bellowed, "Stop!" I nearly jumped off the bench; it actually scared me to death. I turned to look at her and she just sat there, stoically staring.

After a moment, she said she would take me as a pupil, but I was never to bring any of "my" music again. She began pulling out several yellow books with tunes that had no names, only numbers. I looked over the music and it seemed way too simple for me; I felt she was putting me back several years. But my parents were elated, and I began as a student of Miss Lillian Gill.

During the next several months, she taught me how to sit, how to hold my hands and fingers, how to "address" a piano. I had no idea of any of these things. Then she began leading me through practice scales and a few relatively easy pieces, but they had to be performed to perfection.

I began to get discouraged. I couldn't understand why I couldn't play the music I liked and why I was being forced to play music I thought was "beneath" my abilities. One evening, I was making a particular mess of Chopin something or other—I hadn't practiced as I should have—and Miss Gill let the baton come down again on the side of the piano. This time she said, "Move over."

I slid to one end of the bench. She pushed down hard on the arms of her wheelchair and ever so slowly and carefully pulled herself up on the stool in front of the piano, adjusting her legs as she went. She lifted her hands and played the piece for me, nearly impossibly beautiful music. And at that moment, I understood.

It was the difference between a master and a student. After that night, I never confused the two again.

Our Lord is like this when He begins to refine us. At first, we hardly understand what He is up to. But He knows how He wants us to be, and He works to accomplish His goal. He is the Master . . . and we are not.

More Facts about Gold

Gold, represented by the symbol AU from *arum*, has represented prosperity, wealth, and immortality since the beginning of time. It is first mentioned in the Bible in Genesis 2, in the initial description of the Garden of Eden, a land where "there is gold. And the gold of that land is good" (Genesis 2:11–12). Throughout history, it has been sought after for its unrivaled beauty and ability to be shaped into jewelry, statues, and coinage. But over and above all of these characteristics, gold possesses another even more fantastic, inherent quality: it does not corrode.[18]

Filigree, a technique by which metal is pulled into wire and used to create jewelry and art objects, was being used by Egyptians as early as 2500 BC.[19] They also wove gold into clothing. When God gave Moses patterns to use to create the priests' garments in Exodus, He specified gold threads to be worked into the wool yarns of red, blue, and purple. The gold represented God's unsurpassed power and Kingdom might.

In addition, the Egyptians were experts in gold foiling, a process by which craftsmen pound the gold into thin foil and then cover furniture, walls, floors, and other furnishings.[20] The Israelites utilized the technique to cover the walls of the Tabernacle, the Table of the Bread of Presence, and the Altar of Incense. The lampstand was a solid piece hammered out from a talent, or seventy-five pounds, of pure gold.

Later, when Solomon built the Temple, his craftsmen covered the walls and floor in pure gold, and instead of one lampstand, craftsmen hammered ten from solid gold. In addition, the king made two hundred shields of beaten gold, which Scripture says servants carried from the Temple and stored in his palace every evening to keep them safe.[21]

Questions for Discussion

1. We discussed commitment in the last chapter. In this chapter, we learned about diligence. They work in tandem. In many ways, they are two sides of the same coin. Commitment defines the attitude; diligence defines the actions. When have you diligently worked toward something? Have you ever worked diligently toward something but failed?

2. Setting goals is a great way to ensure you accomplish what you wish to do. Someone once said, "The way to eat an elephant is one bite at a time." Can you think

of something you would like to accomplish but lack the initiative to get started? Try making a list of steps you could take in order to start toward your goals.

3. As we studied about God being compared to a refiner and fuller, we saw He has certain goals for who He wants us to become. Can you identify an area in your personality that He may be cultivating right now? What indications are there that this might be true?

Closing Thoughts

God will diligently continue to mold us and refine us until we bear the family resemblance—the image of none other than Jesus, His Son and our older brother. This is an aspect of His love we often don't consider, but He will do whatever is necessary to complete that mission . . . and He will not fail.

CHAPTER 4

A Lesson from Bread, Fish, and Eggs

Extravagant Generosity: Luke 11:9–13, Matthew 7:7–11

Last year, Americans consumed 7.5 billion eggs,[1] five billion pounds of fish,[2] and over forty-three billion pounds of wheat![3] These extraordinary numbers offer insights into our dietary habits. But it says just as much about the convenience of acquiring food—just a quick trip to a local grocery store where the average person may shop for food several times a week.

It reminds me of the new grocery store that was built not far from our house a few weeks ago. When the much-anticipated grand opening day arrived, the entire neighborhood was there—it was like a party! We all agreed the market seemed like our home away from home.

Getting something to eat in the ancient world was drastically different. In this chapter, we will examine a Scripture passage where

Jesus talks about foodstuffs—specifically bread, fish, and eggs—as
a way of visualizing a lesson concerning our entreaties to God.

In order to appreciate the lesson to its fullest, we will need to
examine dietary habits and food production in the ancient world.
What we will discover may surprise you and challenge each of us
to re-examine one of God's most incredible characteristics found
within His love—extravagant generosity.

A Brief History of Bread in Bible Times

The people of ancient Israel depended almost entirely upon
three categories of food for their sustenance: bread, wine, and oil.
And though enough evidence exists to show they used other foodstuffs, these three—wheat, grapes, and olives—comprised the main
crops and therefore formed the basis for life support.[4]

In Deuteronomy, we see references to this trio which supplied
the ancient Israelites their dietary needs for centuries: "He will also
bless . . . the fruit of your ground, your grain, and your wine, and
your oil" (Deuteronomy 7:13). These three have come to symbolize
God's provision for the most basic human need—food. Among
these items, bread emerges as the primary staple.

For some reason, anytime there's talk of bread, I can't help but
think of my sweet mother-in-law, who made the best scratch yeast
rolls you've ever tasted. Many times before she passed away, I would
happen by her house just as she was pulling them out of the oven;
she would butter up several for me, and we would sit and talk. I
miss those times. There is something about homemade bread!

Among the Israelites of biblical times, we need look no further
for a better understanding of the importance of bread in daily living

than the word used for *everything else* eaten at a meal. That word is *opson*, meaning "condiment."

But the Hebrew word for bread, *lechem*, contained the idea of food in general, with bread in particular as the primary substance of meals.[5] In every way imaginable, thousands of years ago, bread deserved its well-known moniker, the "staff of life."

In the Bible, God references bread as early as Genesis 3 in what's known as the "protoevangelium," or first gospel sermon, meaning the first reference to a message of salvation for the world. Verse 19 says, "By the sweat of your face you shall eat bread," pointing to the increased difficulties mankind would encounter in producing food, unlike the Garden of Eden experience, where sustenance was easily obtainable every day.

Archaeological evidence confirms barley and later wheat were domesticated in the Fertile Crescent during the earliest stages of civilization. At first, breads probably lacked leavening agents. And I'll bet you would be surprised to know that as early as the twelfth century BC, Egyptians could purchase flatbread from lean-to stalls lining village streets—the first version of our corner food trucks![6]

In our country today, these so-called flatbreads are resurging in popularity. But ancient-style flatbreads, including Mexican tortillas, Iranian lavash and taboons, Indian chapati, Jewish matzo, and Middle Eastern pita, are still being produced in many societies.

Archaeological evidence suggests the first instances of leavened bread arrived in Egypt.[7] But exactly how leavening was discovered remains somewhat of a mystery.

Yeast spores occur on the surface of grains, so dough made from barley or wheat, if left alone, will rise naturally to some degree. More than likely, through accident or experimentation, cooks discovered a greater rising effect when they mixed a little fermented fruit juice into the flour. Israelites, having spent some four hundred years in captivity in Egypt, would have experienced all these methods of producing flour, breads, and other baked items.

The reality was that procuring food of any kind likely occupied a substantial portion of a person's endeavors. Food historians speculate as many as three hours each day were spent making bread alone. This was mostly a shared process: men gathering and grinding grain, women mixing and baking.[8]

Sometimes bread was baked in crude clay mounds with a hole dug out of the top and a small fire down inside the clay. A round portion of dough would be thrown against the sidewall of the mound and baked. Larger clay ovens provided space for multiple loaves and sometimes were shared by several families.[9]

Clay Ovens in Tajikistan

Food historians say baking bread is one of the very earliest culinary skills mankind acquired. The knowledge of how to bake bread may have evolved out of something as simple as mixing water and grains together, then experimenting with heat.[10]

In ancient times, an oven was a simple clay mound built up on the ground with a fire in the bottom. Then the baker would throw a lump of dough against the interior walls of the oven for baking.[11]

Today, this method of clay oven baking is still used in various parts of the world. Women in Tajikistan utilize the same process daily to produce their family's bread.[12]

Bread was eaten at every meal, and regularly made up the whole meal, providing some 50–70 percent of daily calories.[13] Vegetables were eaten when available, plus figs and grapes—the latter often dried for preservation. Dates and pomegranates, along with a few other fruits and nuts, were consumed occasionally. Wine was the primary beverage, with goat and sheep's milk in spring and summer. Olives were used almost exclusively for oil.[14]

In our day of neighborhood grocery stores, it is nearly impossible to imagine what the daily task of securing something to eat must have been like. Those of us with close ties to farming as part of our heritage may have a more enlightened understanding of the rugged work and haphazard nature of "living off the land." For an ordinary Israelite, however, hunger was part of life—and many times, so was extreme famine.[15]

As we grasp how difficult procuring food was, and how bread played such a key role in the daily lives of ancient Israelites, Jesus's statement, "I am the bread of life" takes on a far greater significance. We acquire a much deeper appreciation for how this statement would have so powerfully impacted His listeners. What He was really expressing was simply this: *You cannot exist without Me.*

A Brief History of Fish in Bible Times

Like producing bread, fishing is a very old human endeavor.

Unlike bread, however, fish comprised a lesser portion of an average person's diet during biblical times. Much, of course, depended on where you lived, close to shore or inland. But even if you lived close to a water source, fish was still consumed less regularly than bread and in smaller portions.[16]

For a place to live and begin His ministry, Jesus chose an area in Galilee, specifically around the Sea of Galilee (also known as the Lake of Tiberias or the Lake of Gennesaret), where fish would have been far more common in the diet. As we have learned, bread constituted the main course, with fish and other items used more as condiments. But we can safely assume everyone hearing the parable recorded in Matthew and Luke had eaten fish, and it probably formed a fairly regular part of their diet.

Still, fish needed to be caught fresh or purchased at market. For people not living in close proximity to water, fish was eaten salted or dried.[17] For those around the Sea of Galilee, the sight of fishing expeditions coming and going would have been familiar. Towns and villages wound like a ribbon all around the circumference of the lake, with evidence of at least several dozen docks and piers jutting out into the water. A decade or so ago, severe drought caused waters to recede, exposing several remains of these structures and providing archaeologists reliable information as to location and usage.[18]

Garum—Ancient Fish Sauce

An ancient recipe for Garum, a popular fish sauce:

Use fatty fish, for example, sardines, and a well-sealed (pitched) container with a twenty-six- to thirty-five-quart capacity. Add dried, aromatic herbs possessing a strong flavor, such as dill, coriander, fennel, celery, mint, oregano, and others, making a layer on the bottom of the container; then put down a layer of fish (if small, leave them whole; if large, use pieces) and over this, add a layer of salt two fingers high. Repeat these layers until the container is filled. Let it rest for seven days in the sun. Then mix the sauce daily for twenty days. After that, it becomes a liquid.[19]

In ancient times, what remained in the earthen jugs then would be strained, resulting in a lovely, amber-colored liquid. This sauce, actually very mild and slightly salty, was used extensively for dipping or pouring over other dishes.

During the first century AD, historians surmise there may have been as many as 230 fishing collectives working the Sea of Galilee. These collectives could be as small as just a few men. However, pulling in the larger nets, whether from shore or out in a boat, required sheer strength, therefore substantive manpower, so some collectives may have contained as many as twenty to thirty men.[20] Several New Testament passages suggest Peter owned and operated a fairly extensive fishing collective employing perhaps twenty men.

If a collective had two boats, that represented a fairly substantial group with a relatively good-sized investment in the business. Two boats were required to use the larger *seines*—nets that would be cast out from one boat then pulled around to form a semicircle with the other boat. Strict tax laws on each catch of fish also required extensive bookkeeping; fragments of some of these records exist today.[21]

A Brief History of Eggs in Bible Times

Let's turn our attention now to the history of eggs. Some food historians suggest domestication of fowl, especially chicken, began in China as early as 1350 BC.[22] And there is some evidence to indicate wealthy Egyptians enjoyed a variety of foods made with honey, milk, and egg.[23]

However, it was not until Roman times that domestication of chickens emerged in Mediterranean cultures, and then only in small numbers due to larger flocks experiencing problems with disease and infections. At this point, pastry chefs in Rome utilized eggs for desserts and cakes. In 25 BC, Marcus Gavius Apicius, a culinary expert of the day, records a type of custard derived from milk and honey beaten with eggs.[24]

Ancient Origin of Deviled Eggs

Wealthy Romans in ancient times often boiled eggs, then seasoned them with spices and sauces. Apicius, in a collection of Roman recipes, thought to have been recorded during the fourth century AD, writes they were served mixed with wine, oil, or broth. At other times, chefs combined the yolk with anchovies to make a smooth paste eaten with the whites. Another recipe called for poached eggs to be served with pine nuts, anise, pepper, honey, vinegar, and broth.[25]

In many Middle Eastern countries, *balut* was also consumed—an egg containing a partially developed bird embryo. Today, in many places, *balut* is still considered a delicacy and can be found in markets throughout Southeast Asia and the Philippines.

In ancient times, only the upper classes could enjoy such costly treats. Eggs were expensive and difficult to obtain.

Up until this time, the only eggs consumed were from wild fowl. These were usually quite small, since they were gathered primarily from birds such as quail, partridge, ducks, geese, and pigeons and, to a much lesser degree, from ostriches, peacocks, and other species. The diminutive size of eggs from all wild fowl as well as chickens is inferred by Pliny the Elder, who wrote that twenty-five eggs were a "suitable maximum for a setting."[26] Columella, the most important writer on Roman agriculture, who lived during the first century AD, recorded twenty-one to be a suitable number.[27]

One recipe Apicius recorded is for boiled eggs. It includes halving them, then mixing the yolk with garlic, pepper, and anchovies to form a "filling" for the whites—a precursor of sorts to the deviled egg.[28]

So eggs, even chicken eggs, were much smaller and far less available than today. Now we use eggs in nearly everything, and picking up a dozen at the store—usually large ones, at that—never crosses our minds as being out of the ordinary.

But in ancient times, eggs were mostly enjoyed by the wealthy and usually used as *hors d'oeuvres* before a meal or as tiny delectables for dessert.[29] The average person may have gone his entire life tasting only a few, if any, as when a small egg could be retrieved from a quail's nest. As a general rule, an egg was a rare treat consisting of a mere bite.

Jesus's Culinary Lessons

For the ancient Israelites, the symbolism of bread, fish, and eggs could not have been clearer. We have three food items discussed in the Scripture passages that, at the time of Jesus's teaching, represented several points on the spectrum of obtainable foods: bread, the primary source of sustenance for most ordinary Israelites; fish, enjoyed less than bread but with some degree of frequency; and eggs, an appetizer or dessert enjoyed almost exclusively by the wealthy.

Now let's look at the pairing of those items with other things. First, in the Matthew passage, Jesus uses a loaf of bread and a stone, and a fish and a serpent. In the Luke passage, He also uses a fish and a serpent, then an egg and a scorpion.

The use of these pairings could refer to the "look" of the items. In other words, a small, rounded loaf of bread might bear some resemblance to a small, round stone. Likewise, there are some fish in the Mediterranean which appear more like snakes than fish. And in the desert areas of the Levant dwell small scorpions that, when curled up, might resemble *balut*.

Jesus may have had these visuals in mind when He drew these comparisons. But since our Lord constantly and consistently used visual imagery as a means of exposing deeper spiritual truths, let's think about what other possibilities they might suggest.

Without question, Jesus's use of bread as a visual here denoted the literal sustainer of His listeners' lives on a daily basis. He begins the message by entreating them to ask, seek, and knock—all verbs of action, all describing actions expectant of a subsequent reaction on the hearer's part. He goes on to say that when a child asks his parent for bread, what earthly father would give that child a stone, thereby denying life-giving sustenance?

But in using an egg as another example—remember that an egg constituted a rare delicacy and treat—Jesus continues to drive home his primary point: that no good father fails to respond to a beloved child's request. In other words, what earthly father would respond with something potentially harmful, even when the child asks for something exorbitant?

What, then, is He ultimately saying to us today? Let's look at five things we can learn from this absolutely amazing passage.

First: Our asking, seeking, and knocking will always and forever get a response directly from the throne of the King of the Universe; each time, every time. We will receive, we will find, we will be answered. Askers receive, seekers find, knockers have doors opened.

But what are we to make of such extravagant promises? Ask, seek, and knock are all action verbs demanding our intentional participation. We are encouraged—really, commanded—to do this. And the comparison includes what seems to be, according to historical evidence, everything from daily fare (bread) to a relatively rare food item or treat (eggs) in the ancient world.

Jesus seems to be saying that regardless of the petition, whether we are petitioning for daily needs or the occasional, rare treat, our Father will not respond with something undesirable from an eternal perspective. By using examples representing a spectrum of food items, He seems to be indicating that whatever we need or want—all the way to something exorbitant like a dessert—we *just need to ask. Leave the answers to Him.*

Second: Answering our prayers is not a chore for God; it is one of His greatest joys. A good father delights in giving good gifts to his children. We have the best Father. He gives the best gifts.

The very best an earthly parent can give to his or her child will pale in comparison to what our Heavenly Father can give. Why? Because all earthly parents, being evil by way of humanity, can never give what God can give, being Holy by way of deity. And the one essential thing earthly parents are completely helpless to provide is forgiveness of their children's sin—*their most crucial need.*

Third: "Ask, seek, knock" seems to form a progression. "Asking" seems more general, "seeking" seems to be more specific, and when we reach a door and lift our knuckles to it, we "knock"—a very specific, intentional action. The progression seems to follow the pattern of items of sustenance: "bread" seems to be more general, "fish" an intermediate item, "egg" rarer and much more specific. It really reminds me of small, medium, and large. It is as if Jesus is saying, no matter the size of your request, present it to God. Small things, big things, everyday things, rare things—take all of it to Him. Present your petitions to Him without hesitation, because He answers—and *He answers without tricks or duplicity.*

Fourth: The use of food as a visual is intentional. Physical food sustains physical life; spiritual food sustains spiritual life. Part of the lesson that is often overlooked in both passages is the emphasis on the spirituality of the asking, seeking, and knocking and the answers given. This is highlighted especially in Luke 11:13, when Jesus says, "How much more will God give the Holy Spirit to those who ask him?"

This is the greatest gift. Let that sink in: *the Holy Spirit is the greatest gift.* Jesus says no matter what we ask or seek, or what door we knock at, the gift of the Holy Spirit outstrips everything we might desire or need.

Fifth: Let's turn our attention now to the spiritual aspect. Here, something must be said about *what* we ask for. Examining how Jesus viewed possessions and our attitude towards them will be key in helping us reach a more profound understanding of these passages.

Gordon D. Fee, in his book *Listening to the Spirit in the Text*, makes this observation: "For Jesus, wealth and possessions were of zero value."[30] In other words, material abundance is neither good nor bad but depends on our view of it. Does material abundance or gaining possessions dominate and control us, or are we searching for something different?

As we mature in our understanding of how extravagant God's love is for us and what He has done for us through Jesus, then our "asking" matures. Why? *Because our "seeking" matures.* The doors that we would have open to us are different doors—they are doors that lead to greater spiritual depth and growth. They are doors to the Kingdom itself.

Does this mean we are not to take requests for needs that deal with life-sustaining things or even things that we would consider treats? Of course not. The overriding sense of these passages is to take it all to the Father—from "soup to nuts" so to speak.

So . . . let us just go to God. Let us just ask Him through Jesus. And let us just leave the answers to His extravagant generosity.

Questions for Discussion

1. Who is the most generous person you have ever known? This could relate to being generous with time, resources, or in some other way. How have you observed that generosity?

2. Would you describe yourself as generous? Explain why or why not. Is there an area of your life where

you need to become more generous? How might you accomplish this?

3. When Jesus stood in the Temple and observed the poor widow place her mite—a coin of little monetary value—into the offering plate, He commented that she had given more than all the other people that day. In other words, she had been generous because she had given all she had—the actual amount was not the point. Are you generous with God? Explain why or why not.

Closing Thoughts

When we bring our petitions to God, Jesus assures us our prayers will be heard and answered. God loves to be generous with His children. As Psalm 50:10 says, He owns "the cattle on a thousand hills." In other words, everything belongs to Him.

CHAPTER 5

The Storehouses of Snow

Extravagant Creativity: Job 38:22

Can you remember the first time you saw snow? If you were raised in a place where winter frequently blankets the ground with white, you probably don't even remember when you initially marveled at snow's beauty. But if you were born and raised in the Deep South, trust me—seeing your very first snowflake etched a special imprint on your memory.

I can envision it like it was yesterday. I was in the fourth grade and I ran outside, so excited I was actually trembling because I knew once the flakes hit the ground, they would probably disappear: Alabama's warm earth is usually not cold enough to prevent these crystals from melting even in mid-December.

Several floated right in front of me, and a few even landed on my cheek. I held out my hands trying to catch one. Then for a brief moment, in my open palm, I saw one of the most beautiful things

I had ever seen—a tiny snowflake in all its lacy splendor. In the next split second, it was gone.

Since that day, snowflakes have fascinated me. And in choosing something to highlight God's creativity, we could easily explore hundreds of different aspects of His creation. The endless variety of seashells, the symphony of colors found on butterfly wings, the shapes and forms of myriad flowers—we have lots to choose from. But few things charm us like these icy jewels.

Maybe part of their enchantment comes from the very fact that their beauty is so fleeting. Consider the observations of eighteenth-century researcher Wilson Bentley (1865–1931), who was one of the first to photograph snowflakes using black velvet to highlight their forms:

> Under the microscope, I found that snowflakes were miracles of beauty, and it seemed a shame that this beauty should not be seen and appreciated by others. Every crystal was a masterpiece of design, and no one design was ever repeated. When a snowflake melted, that design was forever lost. Just that much beauty was gone, without leaving any record behind.[1]

This has to be one of the most extreme examples of extravagant creativity in all of God's world: a tiny bit of exquisite, unrepeated beauty lasting for only the briefest moment of time. Not only that, but the Lord Himself fuels our imagination with a wondrous image when He asks Job if he has ever been inside the Storehouses of Snow (Job 38:22)!

So let's begin by taking a look at the fascinating way a snowflake is formed and then at what we can learn about the Master

Himself from these tiny bits of amazing and exorbitant creations that fall to earth. Hold out the palm of your hand!

Anatomy of a Snowflake

High above the earth's daily commotion of activities and busy people, billions of dust and pollen particles swirl about in the atmosphere. When extremely cold temperature allows, water vapor encircles these tiny bits to form diminutive crystals of ice. As this "seed" begins to fall, additional molecules of water attach themselves to the original, always in a precise, orderly structure: a hexagonal shape, six-sided or six-armed.[2]

Now the "seed" continues its downward journey. Varying amounts of water, combined with subtle changes in temperature, add more variety to the crystal structure but every time in the predetermined, orderly fashion. These tiny gems continue to grow, some requiring a microscope to see; others can be as large as two inches across. Still others melt immediately.[3]

But whatever the size or length of existence, their individual beauty mesmerizes. And within a universe of magical creations, surely snowflakes must rank among God's most breathtaking creations.

Extravagant creativity, all within an extremely orderly pattern, exists to melt away, no more than a flash of exquisite beauty—now here, now gone forever. Unlike other incredible displays of God's exuberant delight in creating—such as the thousands of varieties of seashells that double as homes to all sorts of sea creatures—snowflakes seem to have no obvious function. They form, they fall, they dissolve away.

Of course, when there is great snowfall, other conditions develop. Once on the ground, snow is subject to weather conditions such as wind, changing temperatures, shade, and sunshine. And the range of formations that various amounts of snow can form leads into another magical realm of creativity, including penitentes, sastrugi, megadunes, or cornices, to name a few.

Yet behind all the snow—or as the Lord so poetically calls it, the Storehouses of Snow—lie these little individual jewels, delicate, lacy, sparkling.

God's love of beauty charms us, speaks softly to us, grips us. We could hardly ask for a more captivating subject than snowflakes to direct our discussion of God's extravagant creativity and its implications for us.

Magical Formations of Snow

When the writer of Job used the term the "Storehouses of Snow," it probably was because he had witnessed it in and around Judea, where snow falls a few times each winter. Possibly, he had seen even deeper, heavier snowfall further north in the rugged mountainous areas.

But we can be relatively certain he had never seen some of the truly remarkable formations created by snow in remote areas of our earth, especially places like the polar regions or regions significantly above sea level.

Here, enormous formations such as sastrugi[4] develop, as strong winds blow across the earth's surface, creating parallel waves or ridges. Or, at extremely high altitudes, a formation called penitentes[5] (a Spanish word meaning penitent-shaped conicals) form from wind and freezing temperatures. These elongated cones of snow emerge very close together and often lean toward the sun, resembling an attitude of kneeling—hence their name. Still another formation called megadunes[6] are so enormous in size as to be indiscernible when traversing them. They've only been seen from high above the earth's surface by plane or satellite.

Many other snow and ice formations show the tremendous force and power of God through nature. And just think: All these stupendous formations begin with tiny individual snow-flakes. God must take great delight in what can be formed from His storehouses of snow!

Creativity . . . from the Beginning

The all-encompassing creation passages in Genesis record the beginning of all things. But as we read through these amazing verses, we don't encounter many inklings of what God is really like. We deduce things, really incomprehensible things, but no distinct delineation of His personal characteristics.

However, there is one thing we often read and just as often overlook. "In the beginning, God created . . ." Immediately, we encounter an activity that is not just something God does on a whim or out of boredom. Creating is part of who He is.

The reason we have such a difficult time perceiving God as creativity itself may be because most of us activate our creative juices primarily on the weekends when we search for time to indulge our hobbies. If we are fortunate enough to have careers or jobs that utilize our creative natures, it's generally within a framework determined by the requirements of the business or institution that provides our paychecks. Genuine creativity, then, is something most of us only undertake in our spare time.

Not so with God. He IS creativity, in the same way we say He IS love or He IS truth. In His very existence, He IS creative. Many believe His creating did not end on the sixth day of the Creation account in Genesis, but continues on even now, in the same way His love and truth continues on.

What Does God's Creativity Teach Us?

Let's now study some ways God's creativity teaches us and how these lessons may impact our understanding of His extravagant love.

First: We humans call ourselves creative. We speak of our creativity—"That person is so creative and shows so much artistic ability." When we decide to indulge ourselves—let's say, to create an oil painting—we purchase a canvas, buy brushes and paint, and begin to gather our supplies. Then we go to our studios and paint. If we are good artists, we might say something like, "Look at my masterpiece."

We, and others who engage in artistic endeavors, are displaying our creativity—the innate desire to shape, to mold, to use our creative juices. And each of us, in our own way, is uniquely creative to one degree or another.

God also is creative. We see His creativity in seashells, flowers, birds, and snowflakes. But there is one huge difference between our creativity and His—He never has to go to the store to buy His supplies. He can create from nothing.

Think deeply on that for a moment: God can create from zero, from nada. He speaks—and with a mere word coming from His mouth, creates something. Nothingness is of no consequence to Him. Death is in the same category.

Second: When God creates, His creativity is boundless and knows no restrictions. What does that mean for us? It means that when He creates, He is completely free to mold, form, bend, and twist; and if He deems it necessary, to crush down and start all over. Everything is a possibility, and nothing is off the table.

For example, when a child of God asks for deliverance from something that may be troubling, whether it is physical, emotional, or spiritual, God's creativity goes to work.

Robert J. Morgan puts it this way in his short classic, *The Red Sea Rules*:

> God will deliver His children from every evil work, from every peril and problem, from tribulation, even from death itself. But there are no cookie cutters in heaven. God doesn't have standardized, same-size-fits-all solutions to our various problems. He treats every situation as singular and special, and He designs a unique, tailor-made deliverance to every trial and trouble.[7]

Third: God sometimes employs His creativity to challenge us. How does this happen?

Recently, I watched an amazing documentary titled *American Epic*.[8] The stunning footage shot with the latest cameras and lenses showcased the incredible variety of landscapes across our country.

One of the themes was the hurdles these vast differences in landscape presented to settlers moving west during the 1800s. These demanding conditions, however, actually served to bring out the best in them—it made them stronger, more daring, and actually more creative as they sought to conquer the variety of challenges they encountered as they traveled along.

In real life, God's creativity makes us more creative. Think of the variety of problems we face, the different types of personalities we must interact with, the diversity of jobs and tasks—even our children are sometimes so dissimilar, we wonder where they came from! Each one is as different as one snowflake from the next.

The very fact we must meet these challenges, which carry so much variety, brings us closer in line with the Father's personality. Why? Because we must use our own creativity to handle and cope with so many different people and circumstances. And when we do that, we display one of our strongest family traits—because we are made in His image.

This brings us to our fourth point and perhaps one of the biggest ironies that exists in all of Christendom.

We laud any display of love or truth in human beings, even those with no leaning toward spiritual things. As believers, we do that because we know God is love, and we haven't given up on love or truth, even though mankind has misused, maligned, and thwarted what we know to be God's love and truth.

On the other hand, Christians often seem skeptical, if not downright leery, of creativity in human beings. Creativity has been almost rejected entirely because of the same misuse that occurs with love and truth. In a supreme twist of irony, creativity in human beings, instead of being something that reminds us of our most amazing Creator, tends to cause many believers to shun those who display this most Godlike of all His characteristics.

Artists, musicians, dancers, actors and actresses—just to name a few—fall within this category. Wouldn't it be far better to recognize that when a human being exhibits exceptional creativity, it is due to the fact that he's exhibiting a God-given trait within his or her own personality? It makes no difference whether the person realizes his or her creativity is a gift from God Himself—it is.

Years ago, I taught art along with art history. And many times then and since, I've walked through museums marveling at the fantastic displays of artistic genius in the paintings and sculptures lining the walls. Because I knew the real-life stories of so many of the artists whose works were exhibited, I recognized that many, if not most, do not believe in any notion of a Supreme Being whatsoever. It doesn't matter—their talent remains a great gift from God, instilled in them from the time of their conception. And we can enjoy these works and marvel at the amazing artistic prowess that brought them into existence.

Creativity is as much a part of God's being as His love. We could express it another way: His extravagant love is extravagantly creative. And it is also a part of every man's makeup in varying degrees. We should celebrate that whenever possible.

Our fifth consideration is that what we observe in a snowflake offers us insights into characteristics of God's creativity overall. Everywhere, our Lord's creations display His love of order, His love of beauty, His love of detail, and even His love of humor and playfulness.

Though there is endless variety of shape and size in snowflakes, the basic pattern within the formation of a snow crystal is the same each and every time. As we learned previously, minuscule changes shift the angles ever so slightly, resulting in changes but always within the predetermined order. It is the same with all of God's creations: there is such amazing order—order brought out of chaos.

We also see His love of beauty and detail. Think of the varieties of birds with their magnificent range of color combinations: purples, deep scarlets, sometimes mixed with lime greens, all on the same tiny, winged creature. And if you are looking for created examples of God's sense of humor, go no further than an ostrich or a Suihogan, the "bubble eye" goldfish with its bulging eyes sitting atop large protruding bubble sacs!

Jesus Himself displayed His Father's extravagant creativity. Every miracle was different, if only slightly. Think of it. Jesus never healed a blind man the same way. He never eased the pain of physical suffering twice in exactly the same manner. He touched with His hands, He spit into the dirt to make a paste, He commanded with His words, He prayed over a child's body, He grabbed someone's hand and pulled them to their feet. In one case, someone was made whole just by tapping the hem of His tunic—pulling out His creative power to heal without His actively doing anything at all.

The same is true with sin. In every case when Jesus met a sinner, He dealt with each person uniquely. The basic pattern regarding iniquity was always the same: repent, turn, go, and sin no more. But the individual circumstances in each case varied in actual details as Jesus worked with the person through his or her sin all the way to forgiveness. It was different each time.

Some Final Thoughts

So we come to some final thoughts about God's ultimate creation—mankind. We represent the ultimate examples of God's creativity. We are different in temperament, different in mindset, different in skills, different in talents, different in looks. We are endless in our variety, just like that amazingly beautiful image of the Storehouses of Snow full of snowflakes—alike yet different.

But let's zero in on one specific verse to see if our examining God's extravagant creativity might heighten our awareness when we come across the word "create" in Scripture. For example, here is one that most of you will recognize: "Create in me a clean heart, O God" (Psalm 51:10).

Suddenly, we see the vastness of what that word "create" in the hands of an extravagantly creative God might entail. Nothing would be off the table, so to speak; there would be boundless, infinite ways to answer this single prayer. God would use His total knowledge of the inner workings of the individual person and then marshal all the resources available—an endless array—to fashion a solution tailored specifically for the man or woman before Him.

The question is, do we dare speak that prayer? Now that we see the endless depth of God's mighty ability to create, would we willingly submit ourselves to whatever He would deem necessary to accomplish the cleansing of our hearts?

The endless variety is why each time we listen to someone's testimony about how he or she came to believe in Jesus Christ, we find the stories fascinating—ambrosia to the soul. Have you ever noticed how tailored each story is, down to each detail? The same is true when one shares his or her story of drifting away from our Lord and then being pulled back to His side. Each time, it is the same, yet different.

God loves all His children. Yet, each one He has created with unique temperaments, personalities, gifts, and physical traits. And with each one, He knows exactly what will (please excuse my use of slang here) "float their boat"—not to spoil or to pander, but what will be the precise thing that will either draw them to Him or back to Him. All this He does with every ounce of extravagant creativity at His disposal—and that, my friend, is unending.

Questions for Discussion

1. "Creativity" is a word used to denote a broad spectrum of talents, professions, and gifts. In your own words, define what "creativity" means to you.
2. Think of someone you consider to be creative. Name some of their characteristics.
3. We have been created by a creative God. Think of two or three of God's creations that you find especially magnificent. Now, let's examine what God Himself says about His best and most favored creation. After five days of creating Heaven and Earth and everything in between, He says, "Let us make man in our image, after our likeness" (Genesis 1:26). Spend some time today thinking about the fact that you are made in the image of God Himself. No wonder He declared at the end of creating this world that it was "very good"!

Closing Thoughts

With His creative love, God made each of us uniquely different. No one else is exactly like you . . . and God loves each of us as if we were the only one He created.

CHAPTER 6

The Voice of the Lord

Extravagant Sound of Love's Glory: Psalm 29

Our voices are so distinctive. We answer our phones, and at the other end is someone we haven't heard from in years—and before they even say their name, we instantly recognize their voice.

And think of the different types of voices you've heard during your lifetime: deep, high, soft, flat, gruff, gravelly, husky, nasally, breathy, raspy. Further, with our voices we also project emotions and attitudes: sorrow, fear, sarcasm, joy, excitement, pleasure, arrogance, doubt, anger, and eagerness.

Another aspect of our voices is the tone we use—not just the specific emotion or words, but the inflection we consciously (or subconsciously) interject. It's often not what someone says as much as their tone that reveals the meaning behind the verbiage. A toddler's voice might drive her mom to say, "Stop whining, please!"

But later, a soft word of comfort from that same mother might soothe the toddler's sobs resulting from a pinched finger.

Consider the other activities we accomplish with our voices. We laugh, scream, sigh, yell, whisper, and yodel. And who hasn't marveled at a gifted auctioneer with his remarkable ability to chant and direct bidding?

Then of course there's singing, an endeavor in a class all its own. Several hit television shows with millions of viewers have featured judges who listen to highly skilled performers using their personal instruments.

The Bible actually has a great deal to say about God's voice, about its characteristics and especially its power. Before we focus on God's voice, however, let's begin with a quick overview of the fascinating anatomy He has given men and women that allows us to make sounds of all sorts, to participate in a wide variety of activities, and to communicate in all kinds of ways.

Our Amazing Anatomies

There are three components of the mechanism that generates the human voice: the lungs, the vocal cords or folds, and the articulators. Each is an amazing component interfacing with the other two to create the human voice.

First: Our lungs must generate enough airflow and pressure to vibrate the vocal folds.[1] Even when the lungs are diseased, there's usually enough force to make sounds. Even if a person has only one lung, there's generally enough residual pressure to make sound.

Second: The vocal folds or cords, located in the throat, are the vibrating valves that chop up the airflow from the lungs into audible pulses. These form the laryngeal sound source.[2] The vocal folds themselves are encased within the larynx.[3]

Third are the articulators. They include the tongue, palate, teeth, and lips. Together, these elements articulate and filter the sound coming from the first two components.[4]

On average, vocal cords measure approximately 11 mm in length in women and 15 mm in men.[5] This size difference causes the generally higher tones for women and lower tones for men—yet another example of our anatomy creating differences between men and women, even to our voices.

Now we're ready to examine what Scripture has to say about our Lord's voice. You may be surprised to learn just how many dozens of references are scattered through Scripture describing His vocals—rich and vibrant imagery that suggests some of its spectacular characteristics. It produces a yearning deep within, and we wonder: What would it be like to actually hear the voice of God?

Hearing God's Voice in the Old Testament

Can you imagine the conversations between God and His first children, Adam and Eve? Not only did they hear God's voice, they spent time in His presence.

God spoke directly to them in the Garden of Eden. But after the Fall, things changed. God continued to speak to them, but they no longer experienced His presence as they did before sin entered the world.

Through succeeding generations, many people did indeed hear the voice of God. He spoke to Cain (Genesis 4:6), to Noah (Genesis

6:13 and following), to Abraham (Genesis 12:1–3; 17:1–2), to Jacob (Genesis 28:13–15), and many times to Moses throughout Exodus.

Eventually, however, God began to speak primarily to His prophets, who then relayed these messages to the people. Samuel, Nathan, Elijah, Isaiah, and Jeremiah, to name a few, were men called by God who often heard Him speak directly to them.

One Old Testament person we can be certain had direct ties with God is King David. It is unclear if David heard God's voice in the physical sense, but certainly he heard God speak into his heart and mind many times.

A Psalm about God's Voice

David had a connection with the voice of God from without and from within. Throughout his lifetime, he experienced firsthand God's presence in a wide variety of circumstances, including during the heat of battle, after adultery and conspiracy to murder, under familial duress with children, and in the many joyous occasions when he received blessings.

During all these times, David saw with his own eyes the results of God's voice moving and commanding circumstances. It brought strength and endurance; it chastised and then spoke forgiveness; it comforted and provided wisdom; it accepted praise and glory. This personal awareness lasted until the end of his days on Earth.

No wonder we have a song such as Psalm 29 written by the king, in which the sound of a crashing thunderstorm reminds him of the voice of God. David seems to indicate that he had actually heard the voice of God audibly at some point.

Roaring thunderstorms often swept inland from the eastern Mediterranean, making landfall in the north over the mountains and then rushing down upon the worshippers in the Temple in the City of David. Perhaps it was during one such display of startlingly bright flashes of lightning and accompanying peals of roaring thunder that King David bent to pen one of the most stirring tributes to the voice of the Lord we have in all of Scripture.

Within the span of eleven verses, the leader of Israel lists nine attributes within that surging storm that remind him of the voice of the Lord:

1. The voice of the Lord is powerful.
2. His voice thunders.
3. His voice is full of majesty.
4. His voice flashes forth flames of fire.
5. His voice breaks cedars.
6. His voice shakes the wilderness.
7. His voice makes the deer give birth (tender, sets things in motion).
8. His voice sends out exultation and joy (Lebanon herself skips).
9. His voice strips forests bare (referring to its forcefulness).

David conveys power by using thunder and flames and other catastrophic events in nature to describe the voice of God. But we also see David coupling great tenderness and joy with these mighty images.

However, at the close of the Old Testament, there is a four-hundred-year span when God seems to be silent. Or at least, we have no record of His voice being heard by anyone. Even in the opening verses of the New Testament, the messages heard by human ears are delivered by angels.

There are a few instances in the New Testament when a person actually hears the voice of God from Heaven. One of these is Peter.

Peter's Amazing Recollection of Hearing the Voice of God

One of the most interesting passages concerning God's voice was written by Peter while in prison in Rome, not long before his execution. The big fisherman recalls the transfiguration on "the holy mountain." During this event Peter, along with James and John, literally heard the voice of God the Father proclaiming His pleasure in His beloved Son.

In 2 Peter 1:17–18, he records what happened. And he uses an awe-inspiring phrase: He says the Voice came from Heaven in "majestic glory" (some translations say "the excellent or supreme glory"):

> For when he [Jesus] received honor and glory from God the Father, and the voice was borne to him by the Majestic Glory, "This is my beloved Son, with whom I am well pleased," we ourselves heard this very voice from heaven, for we were with him on the holy mountain.

Obviously, the decades since Peter's witness to the Transfiguration of Jesus had not dulled his amazement at hearing God's majestic and glorious voice!

As the boy Jesus grew, He had to learn to use His human voice. It's hard to imagine, but as a toddler, He probably played around his mother's knees, pronouncing words a syllable at a time just as any toddler must to master language.

Eventually, Jesus used His voice as a human male, and the same magnificent organs of larynx, throat, lungs, and tongue would be used to teach, to heal, to bless, and to cast out demons. As He left Earth, He promised to send a Spirit, a Holy One, who would live inside each believer to guide, instruct, convict, and communicate. And at that moment, the great Voice would dwell inside each believer: the Voice of the Holy Spirit.

Thunder

Though Bible authors use a variety of images to describe God's voice, their favorite seems to be thunder. And who can argue with their choice? Have you ever been caught outside in a really tremendous storm or sat on a porch while it was lightning and thundering until the flashes and noises became so intimidating they drove you inside? A quick look at what happens when we hear thunder brings to life this preferred visual of the Creator's majestic sound.

When a bolt of lightning stretches across the sky, its energy heats the air around it to temperatures five times hotter than the surface of the sun! In a fraction of a second, this heated air expands explosively, generating a shockwave of compressed air. Next, the air rapidly cools back down and contracts. This is what creates the first sound you hear—a high-pitched cracking like a whip, immediately followed by the deep, bellowing rumbles as the long columns of air vibrate in the aftermath.[6]

The Bible writers didn't know the science involved with thunder, but they certainly knew the power that sound represented. God's prophets trembled at the thought of His voice.

Yet Scripture tells us that He can speak to us in a whisper, in quiet and stillness. The point is this—however God speaks, at whatever volume or in whatever manner, His desire to communicate with us has no limitations. It is extravagant beyond measure.

How Do We Hear the Voice of God Today?

How does this New Testament voice of God work? And how do we "hear" it?

There are many who believe the Holy Spirit never communicates with believers unless they are reading Scripture. In my experience, I find that every time I open my Bible, I encounter the voice of God moving, speaking, lifting me through every word, every verse, every story.

But I have also found that during certain moments (far fewer, admittedly, than when I am immersed in Scripture), I "hear" within my mind and heart a clear communication that I know is God speaking to me. *I know this.*

How? Because His words pierce me, cleanly and thoroughly. They are so precise to the moment: they convict, they explain, they amplify with an exquisite clarity, and they always—*always*—align with His written Word, the words of Scripture.

I remember once when I was on a lunch break from my job at *Southern Living Magazine*, I walked into a nearby barbecue restaurant for a quick sandwich. As I entered, I noticed a woman I knew from my church singles group. When she looked up and saw me, she motioned for me to join her at the lunch counter.

It shortly became evident that she was very distressed about something. She shared no details but enough for me to know she was experiencing extremely difficult circumstances in her life. I tried to comfort her by reassuring her that God was with her.

She quietly nodded her head, but then she turned to me and placed her hand around my wrist and her eyes filled with tears. "I know He is, but I wish I could actually hear His voice out loud just once and could reach and touch Him like I'm touching you right now."

I knew exactly what she meant. I had had many moments as a single mom when I felt the same way.

In all the years since I became a believer, teaching and writing Bible studies and participating in overseas mission trips, I've talked to incredible numbers of Christians and heard their unique stories. In all those years, I've only heard one person share that he had heard the audible voice of God. I don't mean that still, small voice that pierces your mind and heart somewhere deep inside your soul. I mean *out loud*.

It was a retired minister friend. During one of his visits with me and my husband, we sat on our back porch, and he shared a part of his story we had never heard before.

He said that as a young man in his late twenties, he sensed God was calling him into the ministry. At the time, he did not have much formal education, was a heavy smoker, and had lived his life somewhat carelessly. He knew it would be an incredible commitment financially to attend college and be trained, to leave the security of his construction job, and to quit smoking—all things he felt he would need to do to fulfill a call to Christian ministry.

As he wrestled with these major decisions, he became increasingly filled with angst at the momentous change of direction for his
life. One night, he cried out to God in prayer and said that if He
was really calling him into the ministry, would He please speak to
him so that he could hear His voice. And this dear minister friend
of ours, very quietly and with his voice trembling, said that for one
brief moment, God spoke and he heard the Lord's voice out loud.

The story was so incredible, my husband and I dared not ask
him any further questions, nor did our friend offer any more com-
ments. We all sat in silence for many minutes, each contemplating
the graciousness and power of our God. We never doubted our
friend's story.

So the question remains: The Bible shows a progression from
one-on-one encounters with God in the Garden of Eden in the
beginning of the Old Testament to a Spirit that lives inside each
believer in the New Testament. It would seem that would make it
extremely easy for us to hear God speak. But if that is true, why do
so many people—so many *Christians*—seem to have such difficulty
discerning His voice?

This reminds me of an interesting story from a Bible study by a
well-known pastor/teacher. It seems a lady in his church, who had
been a serving Christian for many years, suddenly realized one day
that she had never experienced the joy other people spoke of about
"hearing a word" from God. Though she had lived a life of service
to others, her prayers had always seemed to go only one direction.

As she began to seriously contemplate this, there came a day
when she was on her way to a mid-week church luncheon. A
sudden downpour trapped her in her car in the church parking

lot for quite a long time; she had unfortunately left her umbrella at home.

Waiting for the rain to slacken so she could dash inside, she felt compelled to pray. And as she did, she thought about how she had never sensed God speaking to her directly. As she continued to pray, the rain became heavier and heavier, and louder and louder. The thunder and lightning seemed to be right above the roof. She couldn't see outside her car at all.

Her praying became more intense with each passing second. She poured out her heart to God while the rain poured down all around her. Finally, she stopped praying and became completely still internally. And she said she suddenly sensed a still, small voice that spoke inside her mind and heart. "I am here . . . listening to you," the voice seemed to say.

The experience revolutionized her prayer life. Now when she prays, she says she is always fully aware that God is listening. She admits that she does not always "hear" Him as she did on that day during the storm, but she now knows that God can speak into her mind and heart any time He desires.

In his amazing Bible study, *Experiencing God*, Henry Blackaby lists five ways God speaks to us today: through the Holy Spirit, through the Bible, through prayer, through circumstances, and through the Body of Christ, the Church. All five are interwoven and require us to commit ourselves to them. Spending time with God is the only way to know Him intimately—and the only way we will grow to hear and identify His voice.

Look at this comparison between what God's voice speaking into your mind and heart produces and what other voices might generate:

God's Voice	Satan/Others
Stills	Rushes
Leads	Pushes
Reassures	Frightens
Enlightens	Confuses
Encourages	Discourages
Comforts	Worries
Calms	Obsesses
Convicts	Condemns

How amazing it is to think about the voice of God living inside us with its endless ability to communicate! This amazing thought leads us to our next important lesson.

Does One Theme Stand above All Others in the Bible Regarding God's Voice?

The answer to this critically important question is *yes*. Look at the list of Scripture passages below and notice a general theme in nearly every one where the writer is discussing the voice of God:

1. Deuteronomy 5:22—we have heard His voice out of the midst of the fire; also cloud and thick darkness; loud voice
2. Psalm 29:3–9—His voice commands all nature
3. Joel 2:11—His voice commands hosts

Sea of Galilee: This large body of water nearly thirteen miles long has always occupied a significant role in Israel's history. It is the country's largest supply of fresh water and is bordered by fertile farmland. For Christians, its primary draw is its role in the life of our Lord while He was on Earth. Scholars believe this is where He delivered the Sermon on the Mount and walked on water.

Jesus's first disciples were fishermen at the Sea of Galilee. Today, its abundant tilapia supply continues to support a lucrative fishing industry. *(photo courtesy of Dr. Stan Hand family collection)*

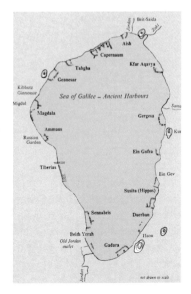

Map of Sea of Galilee: This drawing of the Sea of Galilee shows the sites of fishing docks and piers dating from the first century AD. A recent severe drought left pilings exposed and enabled this artist to mark their locations around the lake's edge, along with towns and villages. Capernaum seems to have had the most facilities and was the home of the disciples Peter, Andrew, James, and John. *(drawing courtesy of Ritmeyer Archaeological Design, Netherlands)*

Almond Botanical: This drawing shows the developing stages of an almond from bud to blossom. *(photo licensed from Shutterstock)*

Gold Refining: Metallurgy is one of man's oldest crafts. Here, molten ore is poured into a mold, called casting, just as was done in the ancient world. *(photo licensed from Shutterstock)*

King Tut's Mask: The Egyptians were some of the most skillful craftsmen in the ancient world. This death mask of the Pharaoh Tutankhamen, comprising two layers of 18- to 22-carat gold weighing more than twenty-two pounds, shows their incredibly sophisticated use of gold to sculpt objects. The Hebrew slaves would have learned all these techniques and carried them into their work creating sacred objects for the Temple generations later. *(photo licensed from Shutterstock)*

Fuller's Field: An early seventeenth-century oil painting of bleaching grounds shows just how much land is needed to spread out large swaths of cloth for exposure to the sun's whitening rays. Biblical historians speculate that fullers needed up to twenty acres to complete the process. The lengthier the exposure, the whiter the fabric became. *(Market Place and Bleaching Field in Flanders by Joos de Momper, 17c., Wikimedia Commons)*

Balut: In many places in the world today, as in biblical times, the half-developed embryo of a chick is considered a great delicacy. Today, street vendors in the Philippines offer two boiled *balut* nestled in a cone of newspaper, sprinkled with salt, for about $3. The top of the egg is broken off and the juice sucked from the shell as if it were chicken broth. Some say the embryo tastes like a regular hard-boiled egg, only crunchier. *(photo licensed from Shutterstock)*

Garum Jars: In 2015, archaeologists uncovered a shipwreck off the coast of Italy containing more than three thousand jars that once contained the ancient fish sauce called garum. Further dating places the shipwreck sometime during the first century AD. *(photo from author's personal collection)*

Clay Oven: These Tajik women make bread today using centuries-old methods. A clay oven, built up from the ground, contains a hole in the middle for burning coals deep within the stone. The raw dough is either placed on a rack over the coals or simply thrown onto the sides of the oven for baking. The hot oven produces a crusty exterior and soft interior. *(photo courtesy of the Dr. Stan Hand family collection)*

Cornices: These ice and snow formations are sometimes well over sixty feet high, stacked up by fierce winds, usually atop an ice ridge. They are often found in remote glacial regions, and if the cornice breaks off, it can trigger an ice avalanche. When located near an ocean and the slide is large, it can cause surge waves or even tsunamis. *(photo licensed from Shutterstock)*

Penitentes: The name itself suggests what they look like—people kneeling in prayer. The tall, slender cones here were photographed in the Chilean Andes, where wind often sweeps snow into amazing formations. *(photo public domain, Pixabay.com)*

Sastrugi: When strong winds sweep over large fields of snow and ice, waves can form across the landscape that are so enormous, they are often only discernible from space. *(photo public domain, Unsplash.com)*

Lightning Flash: Just by looking at a photograph of lightning, we can hear the sound of thunder. It is no wonder that the prophets of old likened the Voice of God to the sound of thunder. Lightning is one of nature's most powerful displays. *(photo licensed from Shutterstock)*

Eagle Swimming: Most people don't realize eagles can swim. They use their powerful wings to beat through the water in what resembles a breaststroke. They cannot launch into flight from the water, however, so they must continue swimming until they reach land. *(photo licensed from Shutterstock)*

Eagle with Eaglets: Eaglets are born with short, stubby wings. But within a few weeks, even a juvenile eaglet may have a wing-span of six feet or more. *(photo licensed from Shutterstock)*

Young Raptor Learning to Fly: A juvenile will spend hours flapping in the nest to strengthen its wing muscles. Occasionally, a gust of wind might catch the young eagle and take him airborne for a few seconds. *(photo licensed from Shutterstock)*

Shells: These small seashells give us an idea of the size of spiney murex, the organism that produces purple dye. Since only a drop or two can be harvested from each snail, it takes an astounding sixty thousand shells to produce one pound of dye. *(photo from author's personal collection)*

Prayer Shawl: This prayer shawl from Jerusalem is similar to those praying Jews have used for centuries. Usually, they are white and trimmed in blue or black, often with the Shema embroidered on the edge. *(photo from author's personal collection)*

Tassel Tradition: A shop owner in Jerusalem adds blue cords to the tassels on a prayer shawl. The tradition dates from Old Testament times, when God commanded the Israelites to dye one cord of the tassels of their garments. The *tekhelet* represents the divinity of God and reminds the praying believer to hear and do the commands of YAHWEH. *(photos courtesy of the Holder family collection)*

Mirrors of Glory: When Solomon built the Temple in Jerusalem, he created an enormous bronze basin for the hundreds of temple priests to clean their hands and feet. It held thousands of gallons of water. Craftsmen also made ten smaller portable basins that resembled carts with wheels. These could be moved from one part of the courtyard to another during the duties of sacrificing and purification. *(photo courtesy of Ritmeyer Archaeological Design, Netherlands)*

Cedars of Lebanon: This recent photo shows the enormous trunk of a centuries-old specimen in The Cedars, a park located in the mountains of Lebanon. We can only imagine how many hundreds of workers may have labored to harvest these enormous trees to build palaces and temples during ancient times. *(photo courtesy of the Jabaily family collection)*

Cedars of Lebanon: Stands of cedars planted within the last two hundred years are beginning to define the landscape of Lebanon once more. Arborists believe that cedars can live up to four thousand years, since they are seldom affected by insects and disease. At least a half dozen specimens still standing are thought to have existed in Solomon's time. *(photo courtesy of the Jabaily family collection)*

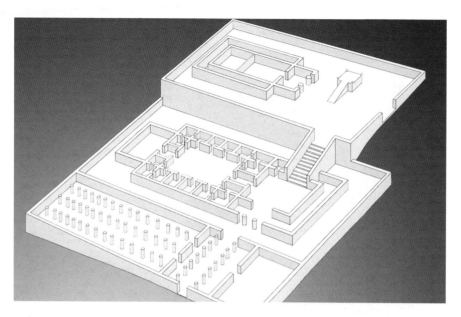

Solomon's Palace: A diagram of Solomon's Palace drawn from biblical descriptions and archaeological data gives an idea of how enormous it was. At the bottom of the floor plan is a depiction of the Hall of Pillars, with its rows of cedar columns. The Bible says the Queen of Sheba gasped when she saw Solomon's palace, and also that he built a similar one for the daughter of the Egyptian pharaoh. *(diagram courtesy of Ritmeyer Archaeological Design, Netherlands)*

Carved Crucifixion: This artist's rendering of the crucifixion is carved into what remains of a large cedar tree in El Arz, originally destroyed by lightning. Lebanon's population is over 40 percent Christian; many of those believers are direct descendants of early Christians evangelized by Peter and Paul during their missionary journey together. *(photo courtesy of the Jabaily family collection)*

Temple Veil: Most scholars believe the enormous veil in what has become known as Herod's Temple may have been sixty feet high and four inches thick due to the heavy embroidery. They speculate that it may have taken four men to pull it back. Knowing its possible size gives us some idea of the significance of it tearing from top to bottom. *(image licensed from GoodSalt.com)*

Soldiers Gambling: This depiction of the soldiers at the foot of the cross throwing lots to determine who would win Jesus's garment shows they recognized its value. The scene also fulfills Old Testament prophecy that His clothes would be gambled away. Psalm 22:18 says, "They part my garments among them, and cast lots upon my vesture." *(image licensed from GoodSalt.com)*

4. Deuteronomy 4:30 and 32–40—obedience to His voice
5. Deuteronomy 15:5—His voice commands what is right, what is necessary
6. Psalm 50:1—The Mighty One, God the Lord, speaks and summons the earth, from the rising of the sun to its setting
7. John 5:37—You have not heard His voice
8. Acts 10:15—voice speaks to Peter
9. Deuteronomy 13:4—obey His voice
10. Deuteronomy 13:17–18—obey His voice
11. Exodus 15:26—listen to the voice
12. John 5:25—voice of the Son of God
13. John 5:30—Jesus says He hears the voice of God
14. Hebrews 3:15—hear His voice
15. Deuteronomy 26:17—obey His voice
16. Deuteronomy 28:2—obey His voice
17. Psalm 95:7–8—hear His voice
18. 2 Peter 1:17–18—Voice of Majestic Glory speaks
19. Acts 22:14—Paul hears His voice
20. Jeremiah 7:23—obey His voice

As you can see, most of these verses dealing with the voice of God concern themselves with one thing—our obedience to it. There is powerful and majestic imagery involving *how* His voice sounds, but the primary focus is always on *obedience to that voice*. Perhaps one of the reasons we do not sense our Lord speaking to us when we pray is that we are more interested in listing our grievances, our wishes, and our thoughts. We're more interested in God hearing *our* voice than the other way around.

Think all the way back to the Garden of Eden one last time. Imagine Adam and Eve actually hearing God's voice, talking with Him, as you and I would talk together if we were in each other's presence. One day, we will experience that thrill for ourselves, and we will hear Him speak—hear His magnificent voice—in ways we will never doubt.

Questions for Discussion

1. What are the hallmarks of a good communicator? Do you consider yourself a good communicator? Why or why not?
2. What are some of the ways you communicate your love to others? Has anyone ever told you that you were not communicating your love to them clearly? Explain.
3. Describe ways God has communicated with you in the past. Are there times in your life when you think He has been silent? Explain why you think this might have been the case.
4. How did Jesus communicate with His disciples? Were there times when they didn't understand what He was saying to them?

Closing Thoughts

When you pray, do you take time to listen? God loves to hear from His children . . . and He loves to respond to them, especially through His Word and the Holy Spirit. He is the greatest communicator in the entire universe.

CHAPTER 7

The Wings of Eagles

Extravagant Freedom: Isaiah 40:31

Last winter, a friend informed me of a twenty-four-hour live-feed camera mounted above an eagle's nest in southwest Florida. Owned and operated by Dick Pritchett Real Estate, the feed has for several years allowed literally millions of people all over the world to watch the nesting habits of a pair of bald eagles in the wild,[1] a species that almost always mates for life. After only a couple of visits to the site, I was hooked.

On December 31, 2020, more than twenty-five thousand viewers, including me, watched as a fuzzy, awkward baby eaglet pushed and pecked its way out of one of the two eggs in the nest. So began a most incredible journey right in front of my eyes, mesmerizing and full of wonder.

I have to admit that sometimes when I couldn't sleep, I would shuffle into my home office, turn on my computer, and just gaze at the tiny, sleeping eaglet. At first, the massive adult eagles took turns protecting their little offspring. They shared the feeding responsibilities, with generous meals of fresh-caught fish, squirrel, possum, an occasional bird, and something that might have been a small cat. They carefully fed him tiny beak bites at first—then as time went by, the young eaglet mangled the carcasses himself, displaying his growing power to unzip prey.

But of course, the one thing everyone waited for with bated breath was the young bird's first flight. And that did not disappoint.

The transformation from weak, little movements to powerful flight began as the young eaglet stretched his wings, usually while lying prone in the nest. But it didn't take long for those soft, gray, cotton-like wisps to be replaced by long, chocolate-brown feathers that formed an impressive span.

Next, he flapped and flapped, exercising his wing muscles while hopping around, always in the safety of the large aerie measuring about five feet across. When winds blew fiercely, I have to admit, there were times I could hardly watch, because you could easily see how the would-be flyer could be swept away before he was ready.

One morning as the eaglet cavorted in the nest, he landed on a nearby branch, a maneuver appropriately called "branching." As he sat there, one of his parents brought him a rather large catfish straight from a nearby pond.

Over the next few minutes, the inexperienced raptor struggled and pulled and stretched, trying to keep that slippery catfish on the narrow branch while he tore off bites. At one point, the fish nearly fell to the ground. The eaglet grabbed it by the tail as the rest of the fish dangled well below the branch.

With tremendous effort, the eaglet finally managed to pull it back up on the branch. Then he awkwardly "mantled" it—the term ornithologists use to describe the way birds crouch over their prey with wings slightly spread to guard it from other predators. Meanwhile, the eaglet was also trying to use his still-developing wings to steady himself. The very large adult eagle sat at the other end of the branch, quietly observing these antics.

But one day, it happened. In brisk winds, the eaglet was flapping about and wound up somehow hanging upside down from a nearby branch—then fell. During the dive, he flapped and flapped, and wound up flying low to a field close to the nest. He walked across the small field and onto a dirt road. Almost immediately, the two parent eagles were there, walking right beside him.

After eating and strolling around, observing the world from the ground instead of sixty feet up, the eaglet flew once more—this time to a dense tree line nearby. None of the viewers saw him for nearly thirty-six hours. He must have roosted in the thick trees overnight. Being on the ground at this point in his development was extremely dangerous, and it made me nervous for him.

Finally, late the next afternoon, with mother and father circling continually around the field as if trying to help their offspring find his way back to the nest, the young eagle emerged from the trees and flew home. I can't tell you the relief I felt when I saw him back in the aerie.

In the days that followed, the young eagle realized he could indeed fly. They were short distances, granted—but he could now sail from one tree to another. He seemed to know to stay close to the aerie as he began to explore the great big world around him. The ability to fly with his magnificently strong wings ushered him into the essence of eagle life: freedom.

Like many of you, I've always loved the beautiful passage in Isaiah when the prophet refers to the "wings of eagles" to make points about strength. Let's read the entire passage, Isaiah 40:28–31:

> The LORD is the everlasting God, the Creator of the ends of the earth. He does not faint or grow weary; his understanding is unsearchable. He gives power to the faint, and to him who has no might he increases strength. Even youths shall faint and be weary, and young men shall fall exhausted; but they who wait for the LORD shall renew their strength; they shall mount up with wings like eagles; they shall run and not be weary; they shall walk and not faint.

I've always assumed this passage dealt solely with strength. And certainly it does—strength from the Lord is one of His greatest gifts to us.

But now that I've watched an eagle transition from hatchling to fledgling to soaring adult, I've observed firsthand what happens as his wings grow and gain strength. That process occurs for one purpose: to usher in freedom. And I can appreciate more fully what the prophet said from long ago.

So let's delve into these amazing verses. We'll begin by looking at what was happening in the lives of the Israelites when they were written.

The Lesser Spotted Eagle

Though some eagle populations remain located in a general area for their entire life spans, others travel great distances seasonally.[2] But few have the extremely broad range of the Lesser Spotted Eagle.

Its overall size may not be quite as impressive as its cousins in Alaska and other northern climates, but their broad, powerful wings, often nearly six feet across,[3] carry them staggering distances twice a year during their massive north-south migrations.

During winter months, these eagles fill wooded areas deep in southern Africa. Then, from late October to late November, they start their journey northward. Using thermal currents to travel sometimes as many as 125 miles each day, they fly as far as central and eastern Europe and southeastward into Turkey. They've been spotted as far west as Spain and France. Satellite tracking indicates some Lesser Spotted Eagles travel as many as twenty-five thousand miles in their wanderings.[4]

Yet these eagles don't nest in Israel. Instead, they fly over the country lengthwise twice a year. Some 90 percent of the world's population of Lesser Spotted Eagles is believed to pass through Israel during their great migration periods—possibly as many as forty thousand a day![5]

The strength of their mighty wings and endurance is unquestioned. No wonder, then, that Isaiah would instruct weary travelers to look up, look at the eagles, and be inspired. The prophet could have chosen few images that would have represented freedom to such an extent as these magnificent raptors.

Historic Background

Most scholars agree that the events referenced in Isaiah 40–54 actually began in 586 BC. At that time, King Nebuchadnezzar II, who had defeated the Israelites in battle, drove them from their homes and marched them toward captivity in the pagan city of Babylon. Now stripped of all possessions and forced into slavery, they faced a crushing future.[6]

Whether God allowed Isaiah, who lived some 150 years before these events took place, to see into the future or whether someone else drew from his previous teachings and then penned these words of comfort doesn't lessen their import. The message of hope comes to us through the centuries, as powerful today as several thousand years ago.

Can you imagine the fear and anxiety that must have swept through the Israelites during the trauma of their relocation? We have a heightened awareness of what such an upheaval might have been like, since in many places in our world today, we witness similar great movements of people as they try to escape war-torn countries or flee oppressors.

As I thought about Isaiah, I imagined him engrossed, as I had been, by a pair of eagles raising eaglets. However, during my research, I discovered a major problem with this scenario: No eagles actually nest in the eastern Mediterranean lands where Isaiah lived. So why would he use their stunning wings and strength as imagery in this important passage?

Now my curiosity was really piqued. Further delving into the subject, I discovered that eagles in southern Egypt and Africa fly to mountainous areas of what is now northern Turkey and Lebanon every spring. Flying mostly near the coastline, they migrate over the entire length of what was ancient Judah—surprisingly close to the route over which the Israelites were marched toward Babylon. These bands of eagles, primarily the Lesser Spotted Eagle, mount thermals as high as fifteen thousand to eighteen thousand feet above the earth. Even today, one of the greatest bird-watching spots on Earth is the Hula Nature Preserve in northern Israel, where thousands of eagles can be seen making layovers during their great biannual migrations.[7]

When the Israelites were torn from their country and forced to march northward in the fall of 586 BC, it is possible that overhead, huge flocks of migrating eagles could be seen soaring, strong and free. The strength of their wings, an undeniable advantage for flying many miles a day, must have been enviable.

The prophet reminded those laboring under the chains of captivity to trust in God, and that out of His strength, they would be sustained. His strength would be their inner spiritual strength. Their spirits could soar through Him even if their bodies could not.

We ourselves may never face the stress and defeat caused by forced relocation—and we certainly pray we don't—but often, the circumstances of our lives are so dire, they strangle our spirits just the same. We feel abandoned and alone. And there may be instances when these events prove so oppressive, they actually seem to steal our freedom.

Was the encouragement Isaiah gave his future countrymen just a bunch of hollow promises, or did it provide a way through their troubles? And how in the world does "waiting," which seems totally passive, infuse us with strength?

Let's look at the entire passage to see what we can learn.

Verses That Set the Stage

To fully grasp what Isaiah means, we need to look at the beginning of the passage where he first reminds the reader of who the Lord is:

> The LORD is the everlasting God, the Creator of the ends of the earth. He does not faint or grow weary; his understanding is unsearchable. (Isaiah 40:28)

Then the prophet lists three specific characteristics of God—from them springs our hope.

First: God doesn't "faint." This word generally refers to a medical condition—some falling away of stamina, or perhaps losing consciousness. The consequence of fainting is not being aware of what's going on around you. But there is never a time when our Lord is not fully mindful of all that's happening, and this applies to what's going on in our lives.

Once again, I can't help but think about the small eaglet and his parents. It is truly amazing how they watched over him. And though they gradually pulled back as he developed, encouraging him to venture out from the nest and begin his journey toward majestic eagle life, they were never very far away at any given moment. The first time he "accidentally" flew, for example, his father almost immediately landed right beside him with a fish, as if delivering a congratulatory treat for his accomplishment. At night, even as he grew older, both parents could be spotted roosting nearby—if not on the same limb, at least in a tree, steadfastly standing guard.

With our finite minds, it is nearly impossible to grasp how God can know each and every thing about each and every one of us at each and every moment. But that is precisely what Isaiah is saying: God stands guard night and day, conscious of all that is transpiring. He is never far from us at any time.

Second: He doesn't grow weary. No matter how swamped we may feel under the weight of our circumstances, God is never fatigued, and this includes never being tired of hearing from us. It sounds almost too good to be true, doesn't it?

Again, I think back to the eagles and the diligence they exhibited in raising their little offspring. One time, during a tremendous storm, the two adults with their impressive six-foot wingspans obsessed over him continually night and day, carefully balling up their enormous talons as sharp as ice picks to keep from injuring their baby, while gingerly positioning themselves over his fragile body to keep him from being swept out of the nest.

When I checked around midnight, I could see one of the adults under the infrared light of the live feed thoroughly soaked, hunkered down, braced against the elements, and the baby completely covered. All through the night, the wind howled and the driving rain peppered down, yet the eaglet remained fast asleep—dry, safe, and warm. What a remarkable picture of watchful care!

Third: Our God's understanding is unsearchable. He knows the backstory of everything, including the hidden past circumstances that may be leveraging their influence on our current situation.

I'm so glad Isaiah added this characteristic. How many times have you wished someone understood you more completely? It may even be someone you've spent an extraordinary amount of time with, like a sibling or even a spouse. No matter how you try to explain your feelings, it seems that person is always a little off somehow in comprehending what you say and what you mean.

Not so with God. His knowledge of us goes to the very core of who we are. He knows every detail starting from the moment of conception—every experience, every thought, and every sensation.

But Isaiah takes it a step further: God understands. In fact, Isaiah says His understanding is unsearchable.

Have you ever said or done something that mystified even you? Perhaps you regretted it greatly afterward, and you cannot even understand why you said that, felt that, or reacted in a certain way.

God understands. He understands all the hopes and dreams that have remained just hopes and dreams—the hopes and dreams that have never come to pass. Yet our trust in Him is never misplaced because He comes to us in the "missed places" of our lives.

Behind all these references lies one underlying point: God's strength cannot be chipped away; it is in place always, infinitely deep and rock solid.

Next, Isaiah lists specific things God does: He gives power to the faint. Any earthly strength has its limitations. We get tired, cross, weary, exhausted. But God, out of His immeasurable power, gladly infuses us when we feel ourselves to be at the end of our ropes.

The Condition and the Promise

Isaiah now moves to his final words of hope and promise clothed in soaring imagery, the heart of his message: He reminds the people that even young men can grow weary and fall, exhausted. There is always a limit to physical strength, and under the right set of circumstances, even the stoutest person can crumble (v. 30).

Then Isaiah sets for them the condition and the promise. First he says, "they that wait on the Lord . . ." (v. 31). Our misunderstanding of the passage begins right about here.

I don't like waiting. Do you? I suspect most people experience impatience when they have to stand in line or sit at a traffic light.

The Hebrew word for waiting is *qawah* (pronounced kah-VAH). It suggests a longing for the fulfillment of the promise of faith: an inner vigil. The vigil is not passive but strongly active.

In other words, it's not waiting without any end in sight. When we wait for the Lord, we stay focused, ready for Him to reveal His plans and next steps for us. It is a kind of waiting that is filled with hope, the certain knowledge of His love and providence.

But there is another way to read this part of the passage. Though the actual word in the original text means "keeping vigil" when translated into English, we can't help but think of how the word "wait" suggests that when we wait on someone, we look after their desires; we consider the things that will make them glad. A good waitress or waiter watches over your table, quietly tending to every need. They serve you.

"Waiting" on the Lord, then, might include considering His desires and serving Him. I can hardly read this passage without thinking about myself in the role of "handmaiden" for the Lord. When we "wait on the Lord," trusting in His plans and watchful care, and when we serve Him—attending to His desires and obeying His commands—our spirits grow in confidence and courage. Following Him brings inner strength.

Eagles' wings truly are amazing. They can span six to seven feet, tip to tip, and provide the ability to glide high above the earth.

Yet, as I have learned, these magnificent wings begin as just tiny, fuzzy appendages with little muscle or coordination. The top feathers grow slowly, and the underfeathers even more slowly. A young raptor looks scruffy for many months as he waits for all his feathers to mature. Then it takes weeks of flapping and practicing to gain the strength needed to fly effortlessly. None of this happens quickly.[8]

We may remain bound to a particular set of circumstances that are difficult and challenging all the days of our lives. We may feel that our feet are forever stuck to terra firma, that we will never be able to soar. But within the steadfast watchcare of our Lord, and as we serve Him, our spirits can learn to mount up as on the wings of eagles. Our inner beings will no longer be caught in webs that hold us back. As we trust His plans and wait for His hands, our hearts and minds will rise up, and we will experience that which can come from our Lord alone—the outpouring of the extravagant freedom found only within His love.

Questions for Discussion

1. Think of a season in your life or a specific event in the past when you may have experienced a loss of freedom. Explain how you handled it.

2. Are you currently experiencing a loss of freedom for some reason? How are you coping with it?

3. Jesus performed many miracles, releasing people from illness, deformity, demon possession, and emotional problems. Essentially, He gave them freedom from these things. But ultimately, God's desire is for us to experience freedom from sin; that's what we most need

to be released from. Do you feel trapped right now because of sin in your life, or is there something you continue to have difficulty with from which you would like to be free? What may be holding you back from seeking God's forgiveness and subsequent freedom?

Closing Thoughts

We may not always be free of circumstances in our lives that seem to hold us back or stifle us in some way, but God offers us the ultimate release—spiritual freedom. John 8:36 promises, "So if the Son sets you free, you will be free indeed."

CHAPTER 8

The Elusive Blue Dye

Extravagant Mystery: Numbers 15:37–41

I often teach a Bible study on the design and construction of those priestly garments first used in the Tabernacle, then later in the temples of Jerusalem. One of the most interesting details involves a particular blue dye used in the robe of the ephod of the High Priest.

The first mention of the blue dye in the Bible, known in Hebrew as the *tekhelet*, is in Exodus 28. When God on Mount Sinai provides Moses with instructions for creating the priestly garments, He commands the artisans to dye the High Priest's robe of the ephod "all of blue" (v. 31). The color blue symbolized "righteous deity," and it still does today.

Later, in Numbers 15:38, God also commands the Israelites to dye one cord of their garment tassels with this gorgeous color; the word "tassel" is interchangeable with the word "fringe," or in

Hebrew, *tzitzit*. These cords reminded the Israelites of two crucial tenets: that God was the supreme, righteous Deity, and that they were to listen to and obey all His commands.

So early in their history, the color blue of the High Priest's robe and the cords of blue in the tassels of the Israelites' own clothing played a key role in their worship. As the Israelite nation grew, it became evident that, due to the incredibly steep cost of the blue dye, coupled with the difficulty of acquiring it, that the cord of blue at the corners of their garments was limited to a single cord in a corner tassel of their prayer shawls.

At some point, the custom emerged for people to wrap the cord of blue around their fingers as they bowed in prayer—a reminder of God's laws and their necessary obedience to them.

Through the centuries, however, Israel was not the only nation or people with a love for the blue dye. Greek mythology tells a story of Hercules walking along the seashore with his dog. After dashing out into the surf and crunching seashells, the dog returned, his mouth stained with blue liquid. Evidently the color was so extraordinarily beautiful, a young goddess noticed it and begged Hercules to use it to dye a piece of fabric and make a gown for her. In return, she pledged her undying loyalty. Archeological digs in Greece later uncovered ancient coins stamped with images of a dog standing next to a seashell—a tribute to the Herculean story.[1]

Evolving Mystery

So for generations, Israelites continued to dye one cord of their garment tassels with this gorgeous blue. However, as the centuries marched forward, a great deal of mystery enveloped the color. Here is how the puzzle began.

Purple, another costly color in the ancient world, was produced from murex—the tiny snails collected from the floor of the Mediterranean. Only one drop of purple dye can be harvested from each snail, so a staggering sixty thousand snails are required to produce one pound of dye—enough to tint a single garment.[2] By the time the Roman emperor, Nero, took the throne in the last decades before the birth of Christ, the purple dye was so expensive and scarce that he banned anyone except the royal family from owning purple cloth.[3]

Most archaeological Bible scholars believe the blue dye came either from another genus of snail or from a formula using the purple dye to create the blue.[4]

So where is the mystery? you are probably wondering. At some point in the history of the Israelites, this legendary gorgeous blue completely disappeared from Hebrew society. Scholars speculate the snail that produced this particular shade went extinct, or the formula used to create it was lost due to the disruptions of war and exile.[5]

No matter the reasons, the ability to produce the color was lost. The Israelites' chagrin cannot be overstated.

The nation has based much of its national identity over the centuries on its ability to obey and fulfill every detail God commanded in the Old Testament. Its inability to fulfill this command so clearly stated in Numbers has created a deep sense of regret for a major reason. The blue cord was absent in the very moments of their deepest interaction with Yahweh: prayer time.

Remember what we read in Numbers about the purpose the tassels served? The key verses, beginning with 39, explain the Israelites were to look at the tassels while praying in order to remember God's commandments and do them. That reminds us of the Apostle James's admonishment in the New Testament to "not just be hearers but doers" of the Word (James 1:22).

The imprint of the prayer shawls, with their glaring lack of blue cords, on the national consciousness cannot be overstated. Such a major visual component interwoven into their daily rituals had been part of their lives since the Exodus as they worshiped and showed adoration for Yahweh, the Lord of Lords, the King of Kings. Thrown over their shoulders each and every day, they served as a reminder to the worshiper, especially the cord of blue, to remember and do all God's commandments . . . to be holy for Him. Lacking the availability of the blue tassels, most Jews have simply used all-white tassels, or in some cases, imitation blue; but neither solution has been satisfying.

As I pondered which aspects of God's love to examine in this book, I couldn't help but think about that mysterious blue, the *tehklet*. How exactly was the dye produced, and what did it look like? And more to the point, why did it disappear? To date, we have no examples of its color, with the possible exception of one recently discovered small piece of faded fabric.[6]

Much has been written about the mysteries of God—about how, as finite creatures, we will never know all there is to know about Him and never be able to comprehend the scope of His being and His magnificence. Volumes have been written about the Trinity alone.

But as I thought about all the mysteries surrounding our Creator, surely none is more inexplicable than prayer itself.

Somehow, it seems strangely fitting that one of the greatest mysteries in Bible history—what happened to the blue dye—should be associated with prayer shawls. Because praying, in all its facets, is possibly the single most mysterious activity we participate in as Christians.

Thinking about the Mystery of Prayer

Have you ever thought about that—the profound mystery of prayer? We can never answer all the questions concerning prayer, but let's take a moment to consider what some of them are.

For example: How does God hear so many people praying at once? Think of that. The Bible says He hears all our prayers.

Next, how does He *remember* every single prayer? That's an even harder reality to fathom. After hearing and remembering, how does He then orchestrate events and circumstances in order to answer specific requests? What happens when two believers are praying about the same issue but asking for totally different solutions?

Why are some prayers answered immediately and others seem to take forever, if they are answered at all? One of our astronauts, after returning from a space mission, said he noticed his prayers during their flight to the moon and back seemed to be answered immediately. His explanation: maybe it was because he needed the answers urgently under those circumstances.[7]

Then the question that perhaps has been asked more than any other: Why does He seem to answer one prayer in a completely positive way—the healing, say, of a child with cancer—but the next child, equally prayed over, succumbs to the illness? Twentieth-century revivalist Vance Havner once said that God writes across some of our days, "Will explain later."[8] We've all prayed prayers that seemingly were never answered.

Furthermore, there are the issues of prayers from God's point of view. Does He have favorite prayers? Are there stumbling blocks that prevent Him from answering?

We have only scratched the surface of the mysteries surrounding prayer. But perhaps it would aid our examination to turn and look at an example of someone known for her incredible prayer life to unravel some of the mysteries.

Study of a Prayer Warrior

Susanna Wesley was known for her deep, consistent prayer life. After her death, her son John said she prayed at roughly the same time every day from the age of seventeen or eighteen until she died at seventy-three. Not only did she have a specific time to pray, but she also usually sat in one particular rocker, pulling her apron up over her head—her own prayer shawl.[9]

This woman had much to pray about!

Susanna was the mother of nineteen children (nine of them died during infancy). Since public education was not available in eighteenth-century England, she formed her own version of home-schooling: she wrote and created simple textbooks and study references for her children and taught them daily. Besides teaching, all housekeeping duties were solely in her hands: sewing, laundry, cooking, cleaning, and bookkeeping. When her husband was away on church business or in debtor's prison, which happened several times during their married life, she handled all magisterial duties related to his congregation—which governing authorities demanded be done with complete accuracy and within specified time frames.[10]

Life was so meager and sparse that crushing poverty often brought them close to starvation. Once, when her husband was yet again incarcerated for debts owed, she said, "Strictly speaking, I never did want bread: but then I had so much care to get it before it was eaten and to pay for it after, as has often made it very unpleasant for me. And I think to have bread on such terms is the next degree of wretchedness to having none at all."[11]

Still, she prayed on.

In fact, there were several things she did absolutely methodically, in addition to having a particular time and place to pray. Susanna would spend several minutes organizing her mind before she began her prayer time. She said that prayers offered up to so mighty and majestic a King needed to be worthy of His listening ears.[12]

She was completely convinced of His presence as she prayed. In modern terms, I've heard people say they often imagine God is sitting with them in the same room or in the empty car seat next to them. Imagining this makes His presence seem more immediate for some. Make no mistake, Jesus Himself said in John 14:16–17,

"I will ask the Father and He will give you a Helper, to be with you forever, even the Spirit of truth, whom the world cannot receive, because it neither sees him nor knows him. You know him, for he dwells with you *and will be in you.*"

So His presence is always within us, whether we sense that or not. Imagining Him sitting near us can help bring that amazing truth into focus.

Susanna prayed prayers filled with pleas for her own inward failings, for God to constantly cleanse and purify her mind and heart. Forgiveness of sin was constantly on her lips.[13] Today, I suspect that many of us go to God with our nightly list of requests and never contemplate just how needy we are spiritually. Our gracious God doesn't turn a deaf ear to the petitions, but certainly there are deep issues within our souls that need attending.

Nevertheless, an older saint I met shortly after I became a Christian suggested one of the most affirming things I've ever done. This wonderful leader at my first church challenged our small group to keep a record of our prayers and their answers. The leader also suggested we pray very specific prayers so we could see specific answers.

At first, I felt awkward doing this, but the longer I recorded the prayers, the more I noticed answers. They didn't always come immediately, but eventually they would. Very few were ever left completely without any discernible answer. This practice did much to strengthen my confidence in God answering my prayers.

Susanna Wesley knew others prayed for her. That is one of the most mysterious components of praying: intercessory prayer. Knowing someone is lifting you up to God is a wonderful experience. And during seasons of difficulty, many people say they knew when others were praying for them—they "sensed" the prayers of believers.

I myself have experienced that many times. One occasion stands out vividly in my mind. The first time I ever shared my testimony with a large group, I was very nervous. I had never done anything like that, and I wasn't sure just how it would go. One of the ladies in church leadership told me she would pray for me the day of my presentation.

As I began to ready myself to go to church, just before the event, I suddenly had what could only be described as a definite awareness inside my mind—I have no other way to put it—and I distinctly sensed that this godly woman was praying for me at that exact moment. Peace seemed to spread over me, and I was no longer nervous. Later that evening, she told me she had been praying for me that afternoon.

Prayer is a mysterious undertaking. But as believers down through the centuries can testify, especially prayer warriors such as Susanna Wesley, there are some things we can say with confidence. They can be summed up in three short phrases:

God listens.

God responds.

Prayer works.

And for all those times when we think our prayers are not answered, there is one amazing verse to remember. In the midst of our prayers, the ones that seemingly never come to fruition, the dreams and hopes that never seem to come to pass, stands John 13:7.

Jesus answered him, "What I am doing you do not understand now, but afterwards you will understand."

Lydia

The dye industry in the ancient world was a labor-intensive business that required vast numbers of laborers. In addition, numerous sites along the shore were required for harvesting, and a large inventory of equipment was necessary to produce the dye and tint the fabric. Although much capital was needed to operate such a business, it had one very desirable component: it was extremely lucrative.[14]

In the New Testament, we meet someone who not only knew all the ins and outs of this moneymaking industry but owned her own company. The numerous workers and sites probably meant she owned two or more villas—possibly one in town and one at the seashore.

With this background in mind, we meet none other than Lydia, the dealer of purple dye, when Paul travels to Phillipi. Her story is told in Acts 16.

Lydia must have been quite a woman. Owning and operating such an important business in a male-dominated world would have required much grit and confidence. And yet, we see Paul singling her out with no hint of hesitation, even though she was a woman. (It's interesting to me that she liked Paul so much. Had such a woman as this detected even the slightest suggestion of Paul viewing women as inferior in some way, I suspect she would not have been so inclined to listen to his teachings and offer him and his friends such lavish hospitality.)

Here's what we can deduce of their obvious mutual respect for one another: Lydia used money made from her dye industry to support Paul and his ministry—and Paul led her and her entire household to a believing faith in Jesus Christ.

An Incredible Discovery

Not long before I began my own research into the mysterious *tekhelet*, professional scuba divers in the eastern Mediterranean pulled up some small seashells that would make headlines around the world, especially among Orthodox Jewish communities.

Some of the murex of these shells seemed to produce drops of a lovely blue color, and biblical scholars immediately began to speculate if the murex that produced *tekhelet* might have re-emerged two thousand years later. You can imagine the buzz it generated across the globe among biblical scholars and archaeologists.[15] I shared these incredible new findings with my Bible study class. One of the attendees was about to travel to Jerusalem, so I asked her if she would look for a prayer shawl for me.

She returned with a *tallit* and an amazing story!

The Search for Blue Strings

Brenda Holder's trip was a wonderful tour with our church, and she took my request seriously. I'll let her share in her own words what happened:

> The quest for a *tallit*, or prayer shawl, with blue strings at the corners turned out to be a long and ardent search for four days in Jerusalem. In checking shops along the way, as well as those in the Old City markets, all the shawls had only white strings.
>
> A little discouraged at the ninth hour, but determined not to return without the shawl, God graciously answered our prayer for guidance. On the most unlikely of days, the Jewish Independence Day, when most Jewish shops were closed, we wandered into a divine encounter!
>
> The shop owner, David, was most gracious and entertaining. He explained, "The strings must be made with hands, never factory-made, and must be blessed by

a rabbi. Then we elevate the *tallit* with blue strings made from snails that have blue blood, since the time of King David." He said he had "authenticated" the blue strings available in his shop, and offered to restring the corners of the shawl.

As his aged but nimble fingers worked, he told us of his grandmother, who immigrated from Ukraine after fleeing the Communists, and opened the shop in 1939. He had worked in the store with his father all his life, and the tradition will continue with his son and grandson. He spoke frequently of the "one true God," and I quoted the *Shema*, which he quoted back in Hebrew with gleaming eyes.

I had asked his permission to photograph the process. He followed a sequence of wrapping the blue string around the white string seven times, then tying a knot, followed by a prayer; eight strings, then a knot and a prayer; eleven strings, a knot and a prayer; and thirteen strings, then a knot and a prayer. He said, "This totals thirty-nine to forty-two blue strings to show blessings God has given us." Our pastor later confirmed this tradition of thirty-nine Jewish blessings.

The shop owner's interpretation of the ancient script on the shawl was limited, since it's a language Israelis don't use anymore. But basically, it means, "Bless you, King of the Universe, for blessing us and taking care of us."

As you might imagine, my shawl is gorgeous! And I've used it while praying many times. As I researched further the recent discovery of the puzzling seashells in the Mediterranean, I found that most Orthodox Jews have long held the belief that once the mysterious ancient blue re-emerges—and evidently, they have always believed it would someday—that it will be a sure sign of the coming Messiah! Many are convinced that the tiny seashells found by the divers are, in fact, the return of the *tekhelet.* So their anticipation for Messiah has greatly increased.[16]

We Christians believe, of course, that when Jesus returns, it will be for the second time. Wouldn't it be just like our God to allow a tiny, humble seashell, deep within blue waters, to begin to emerge once more as an unseen yet glorious sign in nature of that return?

Leave it to our God to be beautifully, majestically, and wondrously mysterious as we pray for His return. As Charles Spurgeon once said, "It seems an incredible thing that such guilty nothings should have power to move the arm which moves the world."[17]

Questions for Discussion

1. You may have heard someone say—or you yourself may have said, "When I get to Heaven, I'm going to ask God about that." Do you have something you would like to ask God to explain to you right now?

2. There are many mysteries surrounding our Lord. What is the biggest mystery about God for you?

3. The Bible makes it clear that one day we will know everything we don't know now. Paul referred to this when he wrote, "Now we see through a glass darkly, but then face to face" (1 Corinthians 13:12). Do you truly believe there will be clear explanations of all that

has happened on Earth when we reach Heaven? How might this change your opinion of certain things?

Closing Thoughts

Believing God is truly good helps us understand that while there is great mystery about Him, there is nothing for us to be afraid of within that mystery.

CHAPTER 9

Mirrors for Glory

Extravagant Purity: Exodus 38:8

Alifelong interest in architecture and building makes the structures of the Bible especially appealing to me. And the first house of God, the Tabernacle of ancient Israel, is one of the most amazing in all of Scripture. The book of Exodus describes the tremendous effort involved with the construction of this desert shrine to Yahweh, Lord of the Israelites. It contained one amazing detail after another, but hardly any as fascinating as the one we are about to study. Here's the verse:

> He [Bezalel, the construction crew chief] made the basin of bronze and its stand of bronze, from the mirrors of the ministering women who ministered in the entrance of the tent of meeting. (Exodus 38:8)

There it is. Tucked into the narrative, after long chapters outlining all construction details of the Tabernacle—the methods, the materials, the measurements, and the minutia—we have this little bombshell added, almost as an afterthought. One of the most important pieces was made from ladies' mirrors. Why would women willingly forfeit their mirrors? Would you and I? And not only that, but these were *ministering* women. What's that about?

We will uncover each fascinating detail that emerges from this one small verse, beginning with the Basin of Bronze, an extremely important element in the overall Tabernacle design. The wash basin, sometimes called a laver, dealt with an issue of major importance to God: the cleansing of the hands and feet of those who served Him. Then we will examine the hows and whys of women who gladly yielded what had to be one of their most prized possessions in that barren, desert environment—their mirrors.

Some Background

First, let's visit the events that form the backdrop for our verse.

After more than four hundred years of captivity, the Lord frees Israel from Egyptian bondage. As God leads them on their wilderness trek, Moses encounters Yahweh on Mount Sinai and receives instructions for the building of a Tabernacle so that God might have a place to live in the midst of His chosen people.

We can only imagine the enormous activity that surrounded this undertaking. Contributions were made, materials assembled, the workers organized.

God then said for each man to contribute according to his heart's generosity (Exodus 35:5). After Moses relates all this to the people standing before him, they leave and go to their tents, then return.

> And they [the Israelites] came, everyone whose heart stirred him, and everyone whose spirit moved him, and brought the LORD's contribution to be used for the tent of meeting, and for all its service and for the holy garments. So they came, both men and women. All who were of a willing heart brought brooches and earrings and signet rings and armlets, all sorts of gold objects, every man dedicating an offering of gold to the LORD. And every one who possessed blue or purple or scarlet yarns or fine linen or goats' hair or tanned ram's skins or goatskins brought them . . . And every skillful woman spun with her hands, and they all brought what they had spun in blue and purple and scarlet yarn and fine twined linen. . . . All the men and women, the people of Israel, whose heart moved them to bring anything for the work that the LORD had commanded by Moses to be done brought it as a freewill offering to the LORD. (Exodus 35:21–29)

Here we have a glimpse at an outpouring of gifts—freewill gifts—from both men and women of Israel as they come to bring supplies for building the first house of God. One of the main pieces God said was to be used in the Tabernacle compound was something called simply the Basin of Bronze.

Constructing the Basin

Let's look first at the function and design of the basin, which God commanded to be placed in a critical spot: between the exterior of the Tabernacle and the holy interior spaces. Read God's instructions to Moses:

> "You shall also make a basin of bronze, with its stand of bronze, for washing. You shall put it between the tent of meeting and the altar [of sacrifice], and you shall put water in it, with which Aaron and his sons shall wash their hands and their feet. When they go into the tent of meeting or when they come near the altar to minister, to burn a food offering to the LORD, they shall wash with water, so that they may not die. They shall wash their hands and their feet, so that they may not die. It shall be a statute forever to them, even to him and to his offspring throughout their generations." (Exodus 30:17–21)

More than likely, several pieces constructed for Tabernacle purposes were created by casting. This meant constructing a mold out of heavy clay, perhaps dug into the ground in the shape of the desired object. Next, workers poured molten metal into the cast, then allowed it to cool and harden. Afterward, artists extracted the item by breaking the mold.[1] These craftsmen probably utilized that or a similar technique to create the basin.

As instructed, the Tabernacle basin conveniently stood between the altar of sacrifice in the courtyard and the curtain of the Holy Place. It was probably about the size of a large birdbath. Since God commanded the priests to wash their feet as well as their hands, the artisans may have shaped the basin with a rim around the base to hold water so that the individual priest could dip his feet in to clean them as he stood beside the basin. His hands could be washed in the bowl portion on top.[2]

The Bible text says the basin was made of bronze, an enduring metal that could be fashioned by the method described above into any shape.

Purpose of the Basin

As stated, God meant for His priests to cleanse their hands and feet during the critical time of service. There were two reasons for this: a practical matter and a spiritual matter. The practical matter involved a sanitary issue. The priests killed livestock as they sacrificed animals, so their hands and probably feet (since they were commanded to enter the Tabernacle spaces with bare feet) would be exposed to animal blood and offal. As a practical matter, keeping their extremities clean would reduce infection and the spread of disease.

But as a spiritual matter, the dipping of hands and feet into water before nearing the altar of sacrifice and entering the holy interior of the Tabernacle emphasized the perfection of God's extravagant purity. Before coming into His presence, the dust and grime of the world must be washed off.

Even though the priests bathed all over before donning their priestly garments, this act of cleansing their hands and feet had to be repeated often during the day as they performed their duties. They must have approached the altar of sacrifice and entered the Holy Place several times daily.

We see this pattern frequently in Scripture. When God wishes to teach us something, we have both of these components existing side by side: the practical and the spiritual. He takes care of us, body and soul.

History of Mirrors

The Bible verse reveals that this basin for cleansing was made from—of all things—mirrors donated by the ministering women. Let's take the details of this amazing little verse one at a time. We will begin by examining the history of mirrors.

Most historians hypothesize that men and women probably first noticed their reflections as they bent over the edge of a quiet stream or still pond. Perhaps they then filled dark containers, pots, or bowls with water as a way of seeing their images.[3]

However, archaeologists have discovered artifacts made from obsidian, a volcanic rock which fractures to reveal smooth, shiny surfaces. These pieces of highly reflective rock have been discovered at numerous archeological digs, which suggest they might have been fashioned into crude mirrors. One area of excavation in Turkey, dating as far back as 6000 BC, has yielded pieces of obsidian which look like crudely made, hand-held mirrors.[4]

As civilizations developed over time, silver and bronze became favored metals for fashioning shiny disks, sometimes even pure gold. Polished to an extremely smooth surface, they offered remarkably good reflections. (The art of silvering was not discovered until centuries later, but the reflective quality of these early metals was quite sufficient.)[5]

Through discoveries in tombs and pyramids, evidence suggests that the ancient Egyptians were particularly fond of their mirrors. They utilized round metal discs, which suggest their favorite deity, Ra, the sun god. As time progressed, artisans added beautifully carved and ornate handles, sometimes shaped as figures and set with precious stones.[6] Perhaps one reason the Egyptians loved their mirrors sprang from their heavy use of makeup. And although mirrors have been found in several modest caskets, even in some child-sized tombs,[7] overall evidence suggests owning mirrors indicated great wealth and high social status.[8]

However, it is Egyptian temple priestesses' use of mirrors that we will focus on here. Evidence from ancient hieroglyphics and other data suggest that temple priestesses used hand-held mirrors, primarily made from bronze, to mark their worship activities.[9]

Evidently, as they sang, danced, and moved their hands to express adulation to their gods, the priestesses used their mirrors to reflect the worship.[10] This practice evolved from one of their deeply held beliefs: that an image shown as a reflection in a mirror lived forever. Therefore, if their worship was caught in a mirror, it became immortal.

Even Egyptian nomenclature confirms this tradition. The word *ankh* means "life," but it is also the word the Egyptians used for "mirror."[11] So "mirror" and "life" are dual aspects of a point of paramount importance in their ritualistic worship—the desire to live eternally.

We can assume that the Israelites living within the Egyptian culture for over four hundred years knew all the customs of their pagan masters. And as the Egyptian priestesses walked toward their temples to worship, Israelite women most certainly observed them carrying their beautiful bronze mirrors with them.

But how did they come to possess mirrors themselves? The Bible tells us that slaveowners often gave them gifts. Perhaps some of the Israelite women owned mirrors as a result of a generous patron. We also know that when the Israelites were leaving Egypt during the Exodus, many gifts of gold, silver, jewelry, linen, and other items were bestowed upon them by people all too eager to see them on their way—the result of the tragic plagues sent by God to force the Pharaoh to set His people free.

However it happened, obviously one of the very few possessions the Israelite women brought into the desert with them were their mirrors. Now we must make some conjectures.

Scripture is clear they willingly gave up these treasures as an offering for the Tabernacle, specifically to sculpt the basin. So we can just imagine in our mind's eye the women leaving their tents, bronze mirrors in hand, walking to the Tabernacle; then Bezalel with his helpers melting them and pouring the hot metal into the mold, which ultimately produced the lovely and critically important basin for cleansing.

Here is the question: Did the women think about how the Egyptian temple priestesses used mirrors in pagan worship? Think about the last detail we discover in our verse: these were the *ministering* women who contributed their mirrors to the basin.

One wonders what their ministerial duties might have been at the Tabernacle. Did they pray and sing, perhaps at the entrance to the inner rooms of the shrine past which only their male counterparts could go? Is it possible that after seeing the pagan worshippers back in Egypt, these women wanted to make a statement about their God—the Lord who had led them out of bondage?

Of course, it is impossible to guess exactly what their thoughts and motives may have been. But we can deduce a few things.

First: These ministering women surrendered something of importance to them—in fact, a very personal item—that, under the severe circumstances of living in a hostile desert environment, might be considered a luxury. It may have seemed like a small sacrifice to us, but for them, it was a personal extravagance.

Second: These women chose to contribute out of their meager possessions in order to participate in a great undertaking. They chose something eternal rather than temporal.

I like to think these "ministering women," after seeing the pagan Egyptian priestesses struggle to breathe eternal life into their worship activities, wanted to express their belief in their Living God. The God of Abraham and Isaac, Yahweh Himself, needed no mirrors to help Him see their worship.

Their Tabernacle was where their Lord of Lords lived. He was in their midst. These ministering women knew His presence was in the Tabernacle and that He was their eternal and everlasting God. Their lives belonged to Him, and His being existed far beyond any reflection in a mirror.

But what the mirrors subsequently became makes this all the more ironic: the basin for daily cleansing. They had no way to know that centuries later, the most prolific writer in the New Testament would further extend the symbolism of the basin.

In 2 Corinthians 3:18, Paul says:

> But we all, with unveiled faces, looking as in a mirror at
> the glory of the Lord, are being transformed into the

same image from glory to glory, just as from the Lord,
the Spirit. (NASB)

And how does this transformation take place? As we constantly, each day, look to God's nature to transform ours, His purity
slowly but surely washes us clean.

Do you recall the story I told earlier about how we are encouraged at my church to pray for a word at the beginning of each new
year?

And as I prayed that first year, I became certain God was giving
me the word "cleansing." I loved my word and spent all year
thinking of all the various ramifications of it.

Then the next year rolled around, and I became convinced God
was giving me the word "purify." Candidly, I began to worry a little.
"Am I in that much need of cleansing and purification?" The third
year, however, I sensed my word was "holy." I decided it might
require two years of cleansing and purifying to contemplate God's
holiness.

As we think about these "ministering women" living in that
harsh desert environment with little in the way of ease and comfort,
yet expressing their love and commitment to their God by relin-
quishing their mirrors to build the basin of cleansing, we are reminded
of the eternal image before us: the image that will continue to transform us until one day, we will no longer be in need of washing.

We have a purifying mirror that we can peer into every day,
and His name is Jesus. We are slowly but surely being transformed
into His precious image.

The Temple Basin

When Solomon built the Temple in Jerusalem, the sacrifices multiplied significantly to serve a growing population. Therefore, the priests required even more water to keep their hands and feet clean. The Lord was not without a solution!

The simple basin made from mirror, about the size of a birdbath, became an enormous "tank of cast metal" (1 Kings 7:23) holding thousands of gallons of water. This new basin was made of bronze and rested on the backs of twelve bronze-sculpted oxen (1 Kings 7:25). At least seven feet deep, it was, for all practical purposes, an above-ground pool!

But the slaughtering tables for sacrifices were located all over the courtyard. So to enable portability of the water, craftsmen made beautiful carts on wheels. These basins were six feet across and held so much water they required the strength of several men to push their carts. These were also made of bronze, with large wheels and beautifully decorated with lions.[12]

However, the principle remained the same. Priests were required to cleanse their hands and feet again at two specific times before approaching the altar of sacrifice and before entering the Holy Place within the Temple.

Sometime during his reign between 744–728 BC, Ahaz, ruler of Judea, removed the bronze basin and placed it in the stone courtyard. Later, the Chaldeans destroyed it (2 Kings 16:17–18; 25:13 NASB).

Questions for Discussion

1. Sometimes we think of sin as having varying degrees of "wrongness." But the Bible teaches that though the consequences here on Earth may vary, sin is sin. Do you find in your life that you view certain behaviors as more egregious than others? Why do we have a tendency toward that viewpoint?

2. God's holiness is founded on His purity. It is perfection without blemish. In your own words, explain what that means to you.

3. The Bible tells us that no one with any sin can stand before the Holy God. If Jesus is your Savior, when you stand before God, all He will be able to see is His Son covering you—the dust and grime of this earth has been washed away, just like the priests when they washed at the basin before the Tabernacle and the Temples. Do you know for certain Jesus is covering you? How do you know this?

Closing Thoughts

Pure love—in other words, love that is not mixed with anything else—is clean, holy, divine, sacred, perfect, unstained, and unblemished. God's love for you is all these things . . . and much more.

CHAPTER 10

The Cedars of Lebanon

Extravagant Strength: 1 Kings 6:14–18

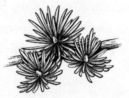

One of the most beautiful components of the southern coastal landscape of the United States is the large and beautiful live oak tree. Just standing in an old grove of these lovely trees impresses one with a sense of strength and might.

Likewise, at one time long ago, there were other trees—cedars—in the northern reaches of Lebanon, covering virtually every inch of that mountainous terrain, trees that soared to the sky with the thickest of foliage and staggering circumferences. So awesome and majestic were these giants that those who looked upon them could think of only one appropriate name for them: the Forests of God.

History and Anatomy of the Cedars

Queen Victoria of England was one of the first to recognize that efforts needed to be made in order to save the great cedars in

Lebanon, lest they risk permanent extinction. Out of her own personal wealth, in 1876, she donated money to Lebanon sufficient to build a stone wall around a 250-acre preserve. The wall was high enough to keep foraging mountain goats from eating newly planted cedar saplings.[1]

Today, the cedars, sometimes referred to as *El Arz* in Arabic by the Lebanese nation, continue to make a comeback. Currently, approximately twelve stands of cedars dot the mountainsides, and recently foresters found four majestic specimens in a remote area of the mountain that are believed to be over two thousand years old, perhaps older.[2]

All these continuing efforts delight Lebanese citizens, whose national flag showcases the silhouette of a cedar. Trees must be spectacular to draw crowds, and these do. Tourists from all over the world travel here to see these historic trees. Just standing next to one is a thrilling experience.

Think back to the days of King David and King Solomon. At that time, all the mountains of Lebanon were covered with these towering giants. We can only imagine what it would have been like to walk among them under their shady darkness, with scattered pinpoints of light piercing down through thick foliage; huge forests of them spread out over acres and acres as far as the eye could see.

A friend of ours at church was raised in Lebanon, and I asked him to describe the cedars. Richard said they were absolutely beautiful to look at but even more breathtaking to stand under. One time, he got caught out in a sudden snowfall and took shelter under a large cedar. He said when it stopped snowing a little later, he was completely dry and so was the ground all around him. "It was as if I was standing under a very large umbrella," he said.

Though some species of trees grow taller than the cedars in Lebanon, these do grow to a respectable height, usually over 115 feet. But it is their enormously large trunks that give them such a remarkable appearance. It's not uncommon for a full-grown cedar to measure over 45 feet in circumference, and often, two of these massive trunks can be seen growing together.[3]

The wood is extremely dense and nearly impervious to disease and insect infestation. Because of these qualities, its superior lumber was highly sought after by nearly all ancient civilizations. Kings and rulers used it for building their palaces and temples. Phoenicians, Assyrians, Egyptians, Persians, and Babylonians, to name a few, sent thousands of lumberjacks to fell the cedars, cutting them down into enormous logs on site. Then, depending on their final destination, workmen strapped the enormous logs together to form barges that subsequently floated down the Mediterranean Sea. Those destined for inland cities would be rolled together and pulled by oxen.[4]

One other characteristic of the cedars made them especially appealing: the incredible aroma released from the cut wood.[5] Can you imagine standing in a huge room with every surface—floor, walls, ceiling—constructed of aromatic cedar with its pungent, fresh scent permeating the air? Often, craftsmen decorated the cedar surfaces with a variety of materials; mosaic, marble, and gold foil were favorite choices. But the workers must also have thoroughly enjoyed that incredible smell surrounding them while they worked.

The heavy pressure on the cedars of Lebanon took a toll. By the 1800s, very few remained. Let's take a quick tour through some of the structures in the Bible that were built from the cedars and just imagine their beauty—a sight that caused one woman, a queen at that, to completely lose her breath when she saw what had been constructed from these magnificent trees!

El Arz

A friend of mine who is from Lebanon shared photos from a trip she took once to the area of Bcharre, where some of the oldest cedars exist. They are known simply as *Arz El-Rab*, or "Cedars of the Lord." In this area, some 375 cedars, believed to be the oldest in the country, grow in a sheltered glacial pocket on Mount Makmel. The surrounding park is known simply as The Cedars.[6]

Besides the great root depth of cedars, the trees have other characteristics alluded to in Scripture. For example, the foliage from each tree in a grove grow together, creating an interlocked appearance among them. Sometimes when one tree dies, the limbs merge into the stronger cedar next door, finding nourishment and continuing to live.[7]

The root tips of cedars also have a special substance that enables them to penetrate stone and dense clay. This characteristic enhances the trees' ability to thrive regardless of the surrounding earth conditions.[8]

Solomon's Temple and Personal Palaces

Let's look at the Bible's descriptions of the Temple to get an idea of just how much cedar King Solomon used to build God's house:

So Solomon built the house and finished it. He lined the walls of the house on the inside with boards of cedar . . . He built twenty cubits of the rear of the house with boards of cedar from the floor to the walls, and he built this within as an inner sanctuary, as the Most Holy Place. The house, that is, the nave in front of the inner sanctuary, was forty cubits long. The cedar within the house was carved in the form of gourds and open flowers. All was cedar; no stone was seen. (1 Kings 6:14–18)

Though Scripture says cypress was used for flooring and olive wood for doors, cedar is overwhelmingly the main wood for the Temple. The last verse of the chapter tells us Solomon was "seven years in building it."

But the house Solomon built for himself took thirteen years to build. Here is the description of it:

Its length was a hundred cubits and its breadth fifty cubits and its height thirty cubits, and it was built on four rows of cedar pillars, with cedar beams on the pillars. And it was covered with cedar above the chambers that were on the forty-five pillars, fifteen in each row. . . .

And he made the Hall of Pillars; its length was fifty cubits, and its breadth thirty cubits. There was a porch in front with pillars, and a canopy in front of them.

And he made the Hall of the Throne where he was to pronounce judgment, even the Hall of Judgment. It was finished with cedar from floor to rafters.

His own house where he was to dwell, in the other court back of the hall, was of like workmanship. Solomon also made a house like this hall for Pharaoh's daughter, whom he had taken in marriage. (1 Kings 7:2–8)

The extensive use of cedar is amazing. And it certainly must have amazed those who saw it in person, because the name given to this magnificent dwelling was the House of the Forest of Lebanon (1 Kings 7:2)!

For such building projects, King Solomon needed an extensive labor force. First Kings 5 tells us just how big:

King Solomon drafted forced labor out of all Israel, and the draft numbered 30,000 men. And he sent them to Lebanon, 10,000 a month in shifts. They would be a month in Lebanon and two months at home. Adoniram was in charge of the draft. Solomon also had 70,000 burden-bearers and 80,000 stonecutters in the hill country, besides Solomon's 3,300 chief officers who were over the work, who had charge of the people who carried on the work. At the king's command they quarried out great, costly stones in order to lay the foundation of the house with dressed stones. So Solomon's builders and Hiram's builders and the men of Gebal did the cutting and prepared the timber and the stone to build the house. (1 Kings 5:13–18)

We now begin to get some idea of the magnitude of this project. Thousands and thousands of laborers were sent to Lebanon for timber. Probably the lumberjacks walked there, or perhaps some were taken by ship up the coast and then hiked inland. Regardless, the trip could not have been easy. Any tools they used, they would have brought and hauled up into the mountains.

I can hardly imagine the work involved to bring down just one massive cedar without any electrical equipment. Everything was done by hand. It probably required several hundred strong men to take down one cedar. And I suspect this work was not without very dangerous aspects.

From Solomon's building projects alone, we begin to understand the reason the fabulous cedars of Lebanon were nearly lost forever.

The Strength of the Cedars of Lebanon

Psalm 92 gives us a wonderful verse using cedar imagery:

> The righteous flourish like the palm tree and grow like
> a cedar in Lebanon. (Psalm 92:12)

And what are the main characteristics of its growth? Certainly strength would be near the top of anyone's list. For every ten feet of cedar above ground, its roots penetrate the earth thirty feet below, the necessary substantial support system for a tree of this size.[9]

Can you think of a more beautiful symbol of the strength of God's love than these magnificent trees of old? Missionary and naturalist Dr. William McClure Thomson traveled extensively throughout the eastern countries of the Mediterranean during the mid-1800s. Inspired by the exotic customs and landscapes, many of which are referenced in the Bible, he published an iconic book in 1859 that is still a mainstay of students studying ancient biblical history.

One of the places that captivated him the most was the mountains of Lebanon, where a few majestic cedars remained. On his first visit, he noted there were probably about five hundred of them left of varying heights, great and small, located in an area about a half dozen acres in size. They grew some six thousand feet above sea level, and some had tops that disappeared into the clouds when weather rolled in.[10]

Though their numbers were certainly diminished from days of old, Dr. Thomson observed that once inside the grove, "There comes a solemn hush upon the soul as if by enchantment."[11] He goes on to describe an overnight camping trip under the cedars. Even in the utter darkness, he could sense the strength of their enormous forms all around him. The missionary stayed awake most of the night soaking in the experience—one he later said he would never forget.[12]

Not long ago, I had just such a sleepless night, but for a completely different reason. That evening, my husband and I had learned a family member was experiencing a very difficult situation. I awoke in the middle of the night trembling with heartache. As I called out to God, I impulsively raised my arms straight up toward the heavens. It occurred to me later that it was as if I had been a little child who had suffered some hurt and reached up to her mother to be picked up and comforted. As I cried out, I sensed just that sort of strength as God seemed to reach down to pull me into His arms to sooth my mind and heart.

A night among the cedars may be memorable. But a night within the strength of God's love during a crisis is one of life's choicest treasures. Surely when we contemplate the enormous strength of God's love for us, we can find no more appropriate symbol than the ancient cedars of Lebanon, the Forests of God.

Questions for Discussion

1. Have you ever been loved by someone, but you suspected their love was not very strong? List ways a person might show strong love for someone as opposed to just talk. Have you loved someone weakly? Explain.

2. Who in your life has loved you the "strongest"? Who have you loved the "strongest"? How were these loves demonstrated?

3. The Bible makes it clear that God possesses a strength of love that is beyond our imagination or comprehension. The Apostle Paul discusses this in Romans 8:38–39: "For I am sure that neither death nor life, nor angels nor rulers, nor things present nor things to come, nor powers, nor height nor depth, nor anything else in all creation, will be able to separate us from the love of God in Christ Jesus our Lord." Do you believe this?

Closing Thoughts

God's love for us is stronger than the Cedars of Lebanon: deeper than their roots, more protective than their branches, larger than their girth.

CHAPTER 11

The Veil, the Garment, the Thief (Part I)

Extravagant Mercy

All Scripture points to one thing—the Lord's Christ and the dawning of His Kingdom world, with the offer of salvation to everyone who will accept it. There can be no greater evidence of God's extravagant love and mercy beyond the story of the cross. In these next two chapters, we will examine aspects of the Crucifixion, knowing it represents the supreme moment of love and mercy, yet realizing we can never come to a full understanding of its mysteries. The cross is the centerpiece of world history: all past events spiraled up to its reality, and all events since have spiraled out from its form.

Let me stop here and share a story that happened several months ago. I was watering a newly planted flower bed in my front yard when two young men walked up. They asked to speak with me about spiritual matters. I immediately stopped to converse, as I always do—I love interacting with young people. These are wonderful opportunities to share our personal faith journeys.

They began by identifying their group and where they met for services. I explained I was a Bible teacher and active member of my church, and that Jesus Christ is my Lord and Savior. They acted as if they hadn't heard me and simply continued on. I waited, then asked them if they would like to know how I became a Christian. Each politely nodded.

So I shared a brief testimony of the years of personal turmoil due to poor decisions leading to loss and sorrow. I told them how, when Jesus Christ came into my heart and life, He filled me with hope and forgiveness through the powerful work of the cross.

They continued to listen politely. When I finished my testimony, the two young men asked if I thought I would go to Heaven based on "just this." I said "Absolutely!"

They looked blank and said, "Just because of what you believe about the cross? There's so much more."

All of a sudden, I felt every hair on my body stand straight up. And from somewhere deep inside me, a sense of utter frustration welled up. I knew there was nothing more I could say to them. So I wished them a blessed day and walked back inside my house.

Immediately, I prayed for the two polite but misguided young men. And I wondered also why I felt such a rise of deep emotion that filled me with a keen sense of displeasure. Then, a still, small voice seemed to say softly within my mind and heart—"Because they said there is so much more than the cross."

Where It Started: The Garden

After Adam and Eve disobeyed God, the Lord came searching for them, asking, "Where are you?" Once they came to understand they could not dwell in His presence anymore, God drove them from their home. To keep them from returning, but mostly to keep them eating from the Tree of Life, God placed a flaming sword "flashing in every direction" to keep them away.

Genesis 3:24 records the scene: "He drove out the man, and at the east of the garden of Eden He placed the cherubim and a flaming sword that turned every way to guard the path to the tree of life." From that point forward, God's presence was no longer available to Adam and Eve as it had been. Here began the great separation between God and man.

The Bible refers to cherubim several times, leading some scholars to speculate they might represent the highest order of angels. The chubby-cheeked angels often depicted by artists, especially during the Renaissance, are often called "cherubim" but don't seem to parallel biblical representations.

We have a description of them in Ezekiel 1 and 10. Here, the prophet describes them with enormous wings and four heads, or faces, emanating from the same body: a human-like face, an eagle's head, the head of an oxen, and a lion's head. Lucifer himself was supposed to have been from this order of angels.

Many centuries went by before God issued one of the most remarkable statements in all of Scripture, Exodus 25:8. If you ever allow this desire on God's part to penetrate your mind and your heart, you will never be the same. With exquisite clarity, the King of Kings says, "Let them [the Israelites] make me a sanctuary that I may dwell in their midst."

In one of my previous books, *The House*, I examine details and construction of the Tabernacle and the Temple, structures which would define service and worship for God's people for centuries. And these structures both begin with these words. In a book filled with remarkable statements, not many surpass the revelation of Exodus 25:8.

> With near-stark simplicity, God proposes plans for a physical place for Him to dwell, and it is exactly in their midst, not removed or at a distance. Ours is the only religion in the history of mankind like this: other deities opt for exclusivity.
>
> Earthly royals have done the same. Think of the monarchs with their castles surrounded by moats, walls, towers, and guards, all meant to keep the royalty in and the commoners out. Kings and queens of England, the czars of Russia, the emperors of China, all went to great lengths to accomplish this. Think of Louis XIV, living miles from Paris, sequestered on an estate where an invitation just to enter his chambers during his daily ritual of donning royal robes and wigs constituted the highest honor of favor. No king ever purposely planned to leave his palace in order to live in the middle of the peasants.
>
> So, in a book filled with remarkable statements, certainly no other strikes us as more incredible. God's desire—and plan—was to come to them, to live exactly where they lived, right in the bedlam of their daily lives. He revealed his heart's desire to be where they were.[1]

But there had to be a separation of some kind, a device that would keep sinful man from entering the presence of a completely holy God—because any man bearing sin would not survive under such circumstances. So God gave instructions to create a veil, handmade by artisans and embroiderers, and it hung between the Holy Place and the Holy of Holies, the place where God Himself dwelled.

Here, the high priest entered only once a year on the Day of Atonement. He carried with him blood from the sacrifice and swung his censor, diffusing smoke into the air so that his eyes would be hidden from looking directly into God's presence. God had created a way for the impossible to be made possible.

Design of the Tabernacle Veil

Cherubim played a key role in God's Tabernacle and Temple design plans. When giving Moses directions for the Tabernacle curtain to be hung, separating the Holy Place from the Holy of Holies, He instructed the embroiderers to use images of cherubim on the veil. These were to be worked into the fine twisted linen in blue, red, and purple yarns.

In Exodus 26:31–33, God says:

> "And you shall make a veil of blue and purple and scarlet yarns and fine twined linen. It shall be made with cherubim skillfully worked into it. And you shall hang it on four pillars of acacia overlaid with gold, with hooks of gold, on four bases of silver. And you shall hang the veil from the clasps, and bring the ark of the testimony in

there within the veil. And the veil shall separate for you
the Holy Place from the Most Holy."

We can't help thinking back to the first separation mankind
experienced, the original separation of mankind from God in the
Garden.

Here is an excerpt from my book *The House* describing the veil:

> This beautifully embroidered swath of linen, heavy with
> its lovely, worked figures of cherubim, marked off the
> most sacred spot within the Tabernacle. The veil becomes
> a symbol for many things: the Holiness of God; the maj-
> esty of God; the power of God; the purity of God; the
> unapproachable nature of God. For the people of Israel,
> the veil did not separate them from a mere godlet, but
> rather the King of Kings, Ruler of the Universe, the Lord
> of Hosts, even YAHWEH Himself.[2]

In addition to the veil, God instructed the artists to use cherubim
on top of the Ark of the Covenant, kneeling with their wings stretched
over its top. Between them was located the Mercy Seat, where God
would manifest His Presence when the high priest entered once a year.

When it came time for the Israelites to disassemble the Tabernacle and move forward in the desert, the veil was used to cover the
Ark of the Covenant. As the priests hoisted the long poles used to
carry it up onto their shoulders and marched through the throngs
to the front of the procession, all Israel could see for themselves how
the Ark, representing the presence of God, was concealed underneath the embroidered linen veil.

So even in transporting the Ark from one place to another, strict attention was given to keeping it covered.

Design of the Temple Veil

Once King Solomon completed the permanent sanctuary to represent the heart of the Israelites' service and worship, a veil once more separated the Holy Place from the Holy of Holies. According to accounts from other historians, including Josephus and later rabbinic scholars, the veil in the Temple was thirty feet wide by fifteen feet high. However, when King Herod remodeled and significantly enlarged the Temple beginning in 19 BC, the veil was purported to be approximately forty feet wide by sixty feet high and four inches thick—so heavy that pulling it open required several men.[3] In addition, Scripture seems to indicate there was some sort of sliding screen to further enclose the innermost room.

The design seems to follow the same pattern as before: long swaths of linen embroidered with cherubim. One account from early rabbinic writings indicates this enormous veil was four inches thick, or a handbreadth, and composed of seventy-two square pieces sewn together somewhat like a quilt. Each square was embroidered with a design depicting cherubim.[4]

What Did the Veil Represent?

Let's look at four elements represented by the Tabernacle and Temple veil. These will lead us toward a greater consideration of what God intends for sinful man.

First: The veil represented man's separation from God due to sin. As soon as Adam and Eve stepped outside the perfect will of God, they could no longer return to His presence. The reason lies within God's holy nature, before which no sin can stand. If a sinful man were to come before our holy God, his immediate death would ensue. The veil, then, was to remind man of his sin and separation.

Second: The veil actually served as a protection so that sinful man would not forget his status and come into God's presence unaware. This second point parallels the first. When God reminds a man or woman of their sinful nature, it is really an effort on His part to protect that man or woman from death—in other words, until they have a chance to relinquish their sinful nature to Him.

Third: While the veil separated man from God, it also did something else: it separated God from man. We almost always think of God as wanting to be separate from us. But not according to that amazing verse, Exodus 25:8—an outpouring of His desire to live in our midst. God's earnest desire was to vanquish the veil as well in order to bring as many of His children home as would come.

Fourth: Whether we are talking about God raising the veil up or tearing it down, both represent an exorbitant, over-the-top love. As I say in another one of my books, only someone who is madly in love with you wants to live in your midst. Once the veil is torn in two and access to God's presence is undeniably available, then we should make all haste to come before Him.

Now we begin to see the overarching importance of this veil, enormous in size and meaning. Next, let's examine New Testament passages to see what happened to it.

What Happened to the Veil?

Three of the Gospel narratives—Matthew, Mark, and Luke—record the tearing of the veil at the moment of Jesus's death. Let's examine what Scripture has to say about this incredible event.

The death of Christ was accompanied by many natural phenomena and miraculous events. In Matthew 27:50–51, the author notes, "And Jesus cried out again with a loud voice and yielded up His spirit. And behold, the curtain of the Temple was torn in two, from top to bottom." Remember, the enormous piece of fabric was some sixty feet tall and approximately four inches thick.

At the same time, the earth shook, rocks split, tombs yielded up their dead, and those resurrected people were seen in Jerusalem after Jesus's resurrection. These events, taken altogether, were persuasive enough to cause a centurion and his contingent of soldiers standing at the foot of the cross on Golgotha to declare, "Truly this was the Son of God."

Next, in Mark, we see an account of the same event.

> And someone ran and filled a sponge with sour wine, put it on a reed and gave it to him to drink, saying, "Wait, let us see whether Elijah will come to take him down." And Jesus uttered a loud cry and breathed his last. And the curtain of the temple was torn in two, from top to bottom. And when the centurion, who stood facing him, saw that in this way he breathed his last, he said, "Truly this man was the Son of God." (Mark 15:36–39)

Luke records a similar account in his Gospel.

It was now about the sixth hour, and there was darkness over the whole land until the ninth hour, while the sun's light failed. And the curtain of the Temple was torn in two. Then Jesus calling out with a loud voice said, "Father, into your hands I commit my spirit!" And having said this he breathed his last. Now when the centurion saw what had taken place, he praised God, saying, "Certainly this man was innocent!" And all the crowds that had assembled for this spectacle, when they saw what had taken place, returned home beating their breasts. And all his acquaintances and the women who had followed him from Galilee stood at a distance watching these things. (Luke 23:44–49)

Some readers are divided about Luke's account, saying it does not seem to fit the time sequence of the others. Personally, though the wording is slightly different, I think it would be entirely possible that Jesus, as He breathed His last breath, could say this just as the veil was torn.

Clearly, the writers' intent is to show the simultaneous events—the last breath of Jesus and the splitting of the enormous Temple veil into two pieces, thereby opening up the Holy of Holies that had been closed for more than three hundred centuries. Charles Spurgeon makes a very interesting observation in his sermon "The Rent Veil":

It is not fanciful to regard it as a solemn act of mourning on the part of the House of the Lord. In the East, men express their sorrow by rending their garments. And the Temple, when it beheld its Master die, seemed struck with horror and rent its veil. Shocked at the sin of man, indignant at the murder of its Lord in its sympathy with Him who is the true Temple of God, the outward symbol tore its holy vestment from top to bottom.[5]

But more importantly, this enormous event of the veil tearing represents an opening up, once and for all, of the Holy of Holies so that all who would may stand before the very presence of God.

The New Veil

Now we will turn our attention to one last sentence, Hebrews 10:19–22:

> Therefore, brothers, since we have confidence to enter the holy places by the blood of Jesus, by the new and living way that he opened for us through the curtain, that is, through his flesh, and since we have a great priest over the house of God, let us draw near with a true heart in full assurance of faith, with our hearts sprinkled clean from an evil conscience and our bodies washed with pure water.

Words nearly fail us here. Scripture not only says that a way has been opened up, but that Jesus Himself is now the rent veil, the curtain beyond which we can enter into a close and genuine relationship with God. But from the time of the cross to this day, that way is *through* Jesus—and only through Him. He is the veil beyond which we regain full relationship with our Father, and someday we will enter into the garden paradise once more.

"Through His flesh . . ." What an amazing thought and symbol. This is why Jesus said clearly before His death that He was the Way. Our admittance into the presence of God is forever symbolized by this spectacular veil imagery: it gives us a symbolic view of God's extraordinary love for all mankind, a way He opened up for all who want to enter . . . *to be able to enter.*

The writer of Hebrews also makes it clear when he says "sprinkled clean" that he is referring to the blood of Jesus cleansing us of our sins. Just as the high priest had to wash before entering the Holy of Holies, so Jesus washes us clean with the pure water of His Spirit so that we may go into the Holy of Holies—no longer hesitant or fearful, but in full assurance of God's mighty love for us, extravagant beyond words.

What Happened to the Temple Veil?[6]

After the Crucifixion, the Temple priests had to replace the torn veil. Perhaps Herod himself led its restoration or directed the making of a brand new one. They may have copied the previous design or created something new—Scripture does not say.

However, in 70 AD when Titus, son of Roman Emperor Vespasian, ended the Jewish rebellion and pillaged the Temple, ancient historian Josephus records the great veil was pulled down and spread out over the ground like a common rug. Then the Roman soldiers piled all the gold plates, tongs, cups, and other treasures on top of it and dragged it off, with oxen pulling it to waiting carts to be loaded onto their ships back to Rome.

At this point, it didn't really matter anyway. Most biblical scholars agree there was no more *shekinah* glory left inside the Temple. God had withdrawn His presence from the Holy of Holies decades before.

After the veil was dragged through the dirt and mire to haul off the Temple treasures, there was probably not much to salvage. Perhaps shreds of the veil could be seen strewn for miles all over the land like scattered crumbs, until finally, nothing more remained of it.

During the Roman siege, the legionnaires built huge bonfires all around the base of the Temple and the foundation walls. These enormous flames they stoked night and day, heating up the porous quarry blocks until they exploded. This was exactly what Jesus had said decades earlier would happen—that no stone of the Temple would be left standing.

The Kingdom of God was dawning, this time in a Temple not made by human hands.

Questions for Discussion

1. The idea of a veil is intriguing: a veil conceals; a veil hides; a veil holds back. It implies that something behind the veil is being protected and hidden for a reason. We know the veils in the Tabernacle and the Temple protected unauthorized people from entering the Holy of Holies—and that kept them alive, since no one can survive the presence of a holy God. Think

of a time when you may have worn a veil. What kind
did you wear and what did it represent to you?

2. The Bible says that at the moment of Jesus's death, the
veil was torn in two from top to bottom. In your own
words, explain what that means to you. What does it
mean for the world?

3. Not only do believers have access to God now in ways
they never did before, when Jesus entered Heaven, He
sent the Holy Spirit to be with us—actually to live
inside us. Think of that for a moment: the Holy Spirit
lives inside each of us if we know Jesus as Savior. *We*
are now the Temple—a body of "living stones." Do you
sense the Holy Spirit abiding in you? Why or why not?

Closing Thoughts

We are no longer dependent on an "external" God; now we
have a God who is as close as our next heartbeat. Take a deep
breath and breathe in the wonder of this.

CHAPTER 12

The Veil, the Garment, the Thief
(Part II)

Extravagant Mercy

During the months of research for my book *Threads from Heaven* (Borderstone Press, 2013), several people asked me if I had learned anything about the clothes Jesus wore while He was on Earth. There is not much to go on, but I will share with you what I have found.

We will begin by reviewing accounts involving the woman "with an issue of blood." The scene is recorded in three of the four Gospels. Here is what Matthew 9:20–22 says:

> And behold, a woman who had suffered from discharge of blood for twelve years came up behind him and touched the fringe of his garment, for she said to herself, "If I only touch his garment, I will be made well." Jesus

turned, and seeing her he said, "Take heart, daughter; your faith has made you well." And instantly the woman was made well.

Mark 5:24–34 allocates ten verses to this event alone. He says the woman came up to Jesus from behind and touched his garments. When this happens, Jesus turns and says, "Who touched my garments?" Luke says the woman came up from behind and touched "the fringe" of His garment. Some translations use the word "edge," others the word "hem."

The people of the ancient world placed great significance on the hems of garments. Clothes represented status and social standing, and therefore revealed much about the wearer. Some readers speculate Jesus's fringe may have had a thread of the *tekhelet* blue. (If you recall from a previous chapter, the blue dye may already have been lost by that time in the history of Israel.)

From examining the articles of clothing typically worn by men of Jesus's day, it seems He probably wore a loincloth under a tunic or cloak, perhaps with a sash, and probably a robe—a vest-like garment that may have been long, perhaps reaching to mid-calf. As mentioned before, He also probably had a prayer shawl.[1]

Ironically, the most the Bible says about the garments of Jesus occurs when Roman soldiers were gambling for them at the foot of the cross. This scene is one of very few that appears in all four gospels. Bible scholars say that when this occurs, it is as if the Holy Spirit is telling us this is a very important event, an incident to pay special attention to and remember. For instance, the miracle of the feeding of the five thousand is in all four gospels, and Bible scholars and theologians give that event significant attention and weight.

So we can assume this description of Jesus's garments to be very important—even more so since it involves the Crucifixion. John gives us the most detail:

> When the soldiers had crucified Jesus, they took His garments and divided them into four parts, one part for each soldier; also His tunic. But the tunic was seamless, woven in one piece from top to bottom, so they said to one another, "Let us not tear it, but cast lots for it to see whose it shall be." This was to fulfill the Scripture which says, "They divided my garments among them, and for my clothing they cast lots." So the soldiers did these things. (John 19:23–24)

Dividing the clothes of the condemned among themselves was probably a common practice for Roman soldiers, but I suspect most criminals had only a few garments and certainly nothing fine. Clothing, in general, was hard to come by in Bible times—fabric, as we have studied, required months of tedious work to produce. So no scrap was ever discarded.

We get the impression that if a person had owned only one piece of clothing, the soldiers probably ripped it into however many fragments were needed for each of them to get a piece. It is unclear in the account whether the four soldiers had already torn some piece of Jesus's clothing to make up the "four parts." What is clear is that when they realized His tunic was seamless, "woven in one piece from top to bottom," they decided not to tear it but to gamble for it by casting lots.

Let's stop here a moment and make some observations. First, what was meant in the ancient world by a "seamless garment"? It did not mean a garment was without seams altogether. "Seamless" referred to a process whereby a piece of fabric was woven from top to bottom in one continuous piece without being taken off the loom. This required a very large loom; it also required great skill since the threads had to be continuously spliced together, using threads of the same quality, color, and so forth. In other words, many hours of labor, skill, and resources went into making a "seamless" garment. Once this very long piece of fabric came off the loom, it was folded over to form a "front" and "back" and sewn together under the arms and down the skirt, with seams on each side. Then, a hole was cut in the middle so that the garment could be slipped on over the head like a poncho. The opening was probably reinforced with an additional piece of material to form a binding.[2]

In other words, Jesus's tunic was expertly constructed, recognizably fine, and very valuable. It was so fine and unique that even rough, battle-hardened soldiers recognized its worth, wanted to keep it safe, treat it with care, and leave it in one piece. Evidently, someone gave it to our Lord because they wanted Him to have a fine garment to wear.

This reminds me of the haunting image described so poignantly by C. S. Lewis of a child playing in a mud puddle, satisfied only because she has never been to the ocean's edge to see the grandeur of real sand and water.[3] These soldiers were playing games, thinking they were getting something "valuable" as the King of Kings looked on, only a few feet away: the One who could have given them any and every truly valuable thing in the entire universe.

Let's press our imaginations further. One of these soldiers that day took home the very tunic our Lord had worn while on Earth. You might say, "Well, it is not a relic to be worshipped."

Of course, that is right. Yet it remained the garment touched by the woman with the issue of blood who was healed. It was the garment that kept our Lord warm all those cool mornings when He sought solitude in order to pray; it was the garment that began to glow with a whiteness like lightning during the Transfiguration; it was the garment He pulled up so that a distraught, kneeling woman could bathe His feet with her tears and dry them with her hair.

Don't you wonder what became of it?

The first movie I ever remember seeing in a theater was *The Robe*.[4] Adapted from a novel by Lloyd C. Douglas and released in 1953, it starred Richard Burton, Jean Simmons, and Victor Mature and was the fictitious story of the Roman soldier who supposedly won Jesus's tunic by casting lots.

I can remember vividly scenes from this film. Even though I was only seven years old at the time, it made a distinct impression on me. The "robe" was maroon and, in the movie, had profound, supernatural effects on all who touched it.

You do have to wonder about the single Roman soldier who left the foot of the cross that day with the tunic. Did he wear it himself later? Did he give it to somebody, maybe someone in his household? Did he ever know the true identity of the One to whom it had belonged?

Many different legends sprang up surrounding this garment. Some say it was "discovered" in Rome around 300 AD and was placed on display for public viewing. Another story suggests the mother of Emperor Constantine gained possession of it and allowed many to view it. In Europe, there have been sightings of what is supposed to be "the robe" as recently as 1996.[5]

But no one really knows for sure what happened to it. The casting of lots for Jesus's clothes fulfilled prophecy written nearly a thousand years earlier by King David, and two thousand more years have since passed. It is one of those interesting tidbits I look forward to knowing in fullest detail someday in Heaven.

Until then, I pray that we never play games at the foot of the cross—that we will always look to Jesus Himself, rather than seeking some material thing He could give us, that it will always be more important to us to *know Him*, rather than something *about Him*.

The Thieves

Next, let's look at an incident that is also recorded in all four gospels, to one extent or another—the two men crucified along with Jesus. Here are the references: (1) Matthew 27:38–44, (2) Mark 15:27–32, (3) John 19:16–22, and (4) Luke 23:39–43.

Let's begin with an overview of the scene.

First: Nearly everyone had deserted Jesus. At this point in the process of His trial, conviction, and execution, there were not many left around the foot of the cross who in any way resembled sympathizers. His disciples had fled, afraid of the authorities and what might happen to them. His other friends also had left, equally terrified of the events taking place. But His mother, with John and Mary Magdalene, were there—certainly heartbroken, supposedly tolerated by the guards because of their familial relationship. But even they "stood at a distance."

For all practical purposes, there was no one left. The scene had proven terrifying beyond what any of His friends, disciples, or followers possibly could have imagined. I suspect they thought something spectacular would happen, something miraculous, at the last possible moment. All through the horrific procedure, they continued to wait for the earth-shattering event that would fulfill their dreams and usher in the Kingdom Jesus had talked about, overthrowing the hated Roman Empire—but it never happened. Instead, they witnessed the most torturous, grotesque, and humiliating end of the man they thought would be their savior and powerful king—and they could not endure it. Their grief, disappointment, and disbelief proved too great. Jesus was alone.

Second: Everyone in the crowd—the bystanders and the rubberneckers—ALL mocked Him, taunted Him, and hurled sarcastic insults. In today's parlance, the crowd surrounding the foot of the cross was indulging in trash-talking and bashing. They felt themselves completely "safe" because the object of their insults was hanging before them, seemingly helpless, so they unleashed their foulest words.

Scripture is clear that both robbers crucified alongside Jesus participated in the verbal assaults, at least at first. In Matthew 27:44, after giving specific examples of the insults bystanders were hurling at Jesus, the writer says: "And the robbers who were crucified with him also reviled him in the same way."

Third: Jesus was, humanly speaking, at His weakest. He was in horrible pain, suffering anguish for all the world to see, naked and abandoned. From all *outward* appearances, He had no power, no authority, no friends or support of any kind. At this point, there was nothing at all to indicate anything remotely resembling kingship or deity. Nothing. He was bloody, sweaty, smelly, hurting, alone, and most undeniably dying.

So if the thief who began by deriding Him for several of those fateful hours then turned to give what some call the greatest testament of faith in the entire Bible, what happened to make that robber change His mind? Remember, he began by participating in the derision, the mocking, the spitting, all of that. Yet, after hanging next to Jesus for a few hours, he turned and gave an unbelievably beautiful and complete witness. What happened?

The Listening Stranger

We have all heard of what soldiers call a "foxhole conversion"—meaning when a soldier hunkers down in a foxhole in the heat of battle, gripped with an understanding of just how mortal he really is, often he calls out to God in those moments of fear, pain, and anguish.

And while that certainly describes the situation the thief was in, there were also many other remarkable things going on around him. Let's consider his immediate surroundings during the last hours of his life to see if we can identify some of the things he may have experienced and witnessed.

First: The thief heard everything Jesus was saying, and the only words He uttered were words of love and mercy—really extravagant words and exorbitant declarations of love and mercy. Remember our dictionary definition of "extravagant" we talked about at the beginning of this book?

> extravagant (ik-stra-vi-gənt): *adj.* exceeding the limits of reason; extremely elaborate; lacking in restraint. Synonyms: profuse, lavish, bountiful.

The thief hears no word of hatred, anger, or nastiness of any sort—in fact, just the opposite: words of kindness, forgiveness, gentleness . . . only utterances of mercy from this man hanging next to him.

Second: The thief witnessed Jesus executing His familial responsibilities to the extent He could under the circumstances. Jesus announces to John that now he will be His mother's son and Mary will be John's mother. Jesus relinquishes the care of His mother to a trusted friend. But he also gives John a mother, something he evidently didn't have at that point in his life—and what a mother! The woman chosen by God to be the mother to His own Son!

Perhaps the thief, when he witnesses this poignant familial love, thinks about his own mother. Who would not do that under similar circumstances? What stands out for us is how Jesus was thinking of someone else and their welfare, not His own: making arrangements for her and doing what He could to ensure Mary's continued wellbeing after He was gone. Even in His agony, He was tending to His responsibilities.

I suspect John tightened his hold around Mary's shoulders at those words, assuring her of his intention to fulfill this dying wish. The thief witnessed all this and understood what was taking place.

Third: In one of Charles Spurgeon's great sermons on the Crucifixion, he points out that more than likely the thief could see the sign attached to the cross above Jesus's head. So he would have read for himself the declaration of who He was: "Jesus of Nazareth, King of the Jews" (John 19:19).[6]

Scripture tells us that Pontius Pilate ordered the sign constructed and chose the words. He also commanded it be written in three languages—Hebrew, Aramaic, and Greek.

We will stop here a moment. Until I began taking a very close look at the aspects of this scene in light of what we are studying, it never occurred to me that the thief on the cross could see this sign. Even if he couldn't see it after it was nailed in place, more than likely he heard the Pharisees arguing with the Roman soldiers about what it should say. The Jewish leaders absolutely did not want this message printed and displayed before the world.

As I pondered this, I began to think about the power of the written word—especially the words written under the authority of the Holy Spirit. And suddenly it occurred to me: since these were the very first words ever written about Jesus after He came to Earth—the entire Old Testament was written *before* Jesus was born, and the entire New Testament was written *after* His death and resurrection—they are truly the first *recorded* words of the New Covenant. And, irony of ironies, they were written by Pontius Pilate! You could think of this sign as a tiny New Testament Bible summed up in one verse!

It was certainly the only "Scripture" the thief ever read or had access to about Jesus—and yet it told him everything he needed to know: "Jesus of Nazareth, King of the Jews." The robber had one phrase about the man hanging next to him, and it said everything. Perhaps it spoke to his soul as surely as verses in Scripture we read speak to us today.

Fourth: The thief saw what forgiveness really looked like. This part of Jesus's demeanor must have been stunning, shocking, incomprehensible. That a man could endure so much pain with only mercy in his heart for those who were *causing* it is nearly beyond what we can comprehend ourselves. But to have witnessed that in the very moment it was happening had to have been overwhelming.

"Father, forgive them," said Jesus. Surely when the thief heard that, he also picked up on the fact that Jesus was in deep conversation with some unseen force or spirit—someone or something beyond the immediate scene. And He addressed this unseen force or spirit as "Father."

Then comes the next startling statement. "They don't realize what they are doing." This represents a total release of responsibility from their actions for all these people—the soldiers, the leaders, the scoffers, the mockers. This man, Jesus, was asking for the people who were torturing Him to death to be released from bearing any responsibility for their deeds. The attitude represents such extravagant mercy that it's nearly impossible to get our minds around it.

Fifth: This next point I've wondered about ever since I became a Christian at the age of thirty. When Jesus first approached Peter and the others who were fishing to recruit them, the Bible tells us they simply threw down their nets and followed Him. They immediately quit their jobs, left everything behind, and followed without knowing where they were going or even who Jesus was. That, my friend, is charisma. That's "I don't know who He is, but there's just something about Him that's irresistible."

Time and again, in the stories about Jesus, we see this phenomenon. His very presence must have been mesmerizing. He spoke with absolute authority, with total confidence. He never wavered or second-guessed anything. He never had a moment of indecision. Every word that ever came out of His mouth and everything He did was deliberate. He never got up in the morning and said, "I wonder what I'm going to do today." Or when some desperate thing happened, He never said, "I don't know what to do." Absolute authority and confidence permeated all His actions, thoughts, and words.

And I'm certain it was the same at the cross. The mesmerizing presence of Jesus, the man, had to have been at its zenith there. In His moment of greatest apparent weakness, He must still have exuded the power of life and absolute authority itself.

The hurting and pitiful thief, whose name and offense we don't even know beyond the fact that he had stolen something, witnessed all this closely enough to hear each of Jesus's agonizing breaths. Yet the Lord's magnificent presence, continuing to drip with extravagance, could not be denied.

The Turning Point

So the thief continues to listen and watch all that is going on from what can only be described as his completely unfortunate ringside seat. But something begins to stir within his heart. Our first hint that something is happening internally to this man begins with a rebuke of the third person within earshot—the thief on the other side of Jesus.

In a last-ditch act of desperation, he dares Jesus to save all of them. Mockingly, he yells, "Are you not the Christ? Save yourself and us!"

At this juncture, our first thief says a remarkable thing. "Do you not fear God?" The answer is framed within the question. The thief already knows or at least suspects it. What he is really saying is, "It's obvious to me that you do not fear God." But within that question is an underlying admission on his part—that *God is Lord over life and to be feared.*

Scripture tells us that the beginning of wisdom is fear of the Lord. Here we have a recognition of who God is and the beginning of the proper respect for His authority. We also see a man who has squandered his life coming into wisdom—the beginning of a deeper vision of life than he ever possessed before.

The second sentence shows the nucleus of confession. The thief says that he and the other man are both receiving what they deserve for their misdeeds. The Bible says, "If we are faithful to confess our sins, He is faithful to forgive us"(1 John 1:9)—regardless of how late the confession may be in coming. This is a confession of sin by the thief. So begins his turn toward sinlessness.

Then he makes a simple, amazing statement: "This man has done nothing wrong." Spurgeon says the statement is all-inclusive. Not only is Jesus not guilty of the offense of which he is charged, He is not guilty of *anything*—no wrongdoing at all. Within this humble phrase, we actually have a magnificent declaration of perhaps the most complex issue in all of history: Jesus was a perfect, sinless *man*.[7]

Finally, the thief says to Jesus, "Remember me when you enter your kingdom." There is so much here, my dear reader.

The thief acknowledges that Jesus has a Kingdom somewhere—a confession that indicates Jesus is royalty because only a king has a kingdom, right? The start of each individual's walk with Jesus begins here—acknowledging His Kingship.

Next, the dying man admits he wants to be a part of whatever Jesus is part of. If you think about it, that may be the most amazing thing he says. Something within the thief must have affirmed that, regardless of what life on Earth had taught him thus far, there must be something better than what he had experienced. And whatever that "something better" was, the thief realized that this Jesus knew the way to get to it.

So the nameless thief says, "Remember me when you come into your kingdom." With so little life remaining in him, he is suddenly infused with what will turn out to be life everlasting. I feel absolutely certain that this poor man really had no idea where or what he was going to—but just listening to the man hanging next to him and hearing His unbelievably kind, powerful, and gracious words was enough to make the thief desire to be with Him wherever He wound up.

You know, the thief had that part exactly right. If all we have in Heaven is Jesus, that will be enough. For that matter, if all we have in this life is Jesus, that is also enough. For if the King remembers you, you are remembered indeed.

Final Thoughts

I stated at the beginning of this book that any talk of extravagant love should begin and end with the Lord Jesus; that to understand the fullness of His love, it helps to examine various aspects of it. So we have studied the amazing thoughtfulness of His love for us and His commitment and diligence to hold on to us; looking at how Jesus taught us to pray reveals the depth of His generosity toward us; thinking of His creativity helps us understand that His ability to work with us and through us is limitless. Knowing that each of us represents a unique being in His universe helps us understand a little more how much He desires to communicate with us and the freedom we have within His love.

As with any truly remarkable love, there is always mystery, and He will forever be beyond our complete comprehension until we are with Him. His purity has no measure, and only by looking into the mirror of Jesus do we begin to see where we need to be. His love is not weak, but strong beyond imagining. Finally, there is mercy in this love of His for us—abiding, deep mercy, like the Lover that He is, wooing us, watching us, waiting for us. We sin the same sin, and when we come to Him and say, "Please forgive me again, Lord," He always answers, "I forgive you . . . again." Mercy is at the center of His love for mankind.

But let's take just another moment to visit the last scene before Jesus dies on the cross and what He says to the thief next to Him. After the thief's simple yet profound confessions, Jesus announces this utterly astounding thing: "Today, you will be with me in paradise."

Oh my, what a statement! If Jesus died during the ninth hour (three o'clock in the afternoon), which is the time stated in the Bible, then the thief died the same day, because Jesus clearly says *that day* they would be together. Scripture goes on to show us how the Roman soldiers hastened the thieves' deaths by breaking their legs—but Jesus had already passed, so His body they left intact other than to stab Him in the side with a spear to make sure He was really dead.

Now it appears that this man—this thief—was the last sinner on Earth to accept Jesus's gift of forgiveness and redemption before He died. You may recall that earlier, a Roman soldier, after hearing Jesus ask that they all be forgiven, exclaimed that He must indeed be the Son of God.

But the thief was the last *convert* before Jesus entered His Kingdom, which He said clearly He would do *that day*.

Here is where my imagination starts kicking in. Can't you just envision all of Heaven—all the angels and cherubim, all the hosts and heavenly beings—breathlessly waiting for the return of their

King? Hundreds of thousands of them waiting for that moment. Then there is a sudden hush, and in the distance, they see His form walking toward them. It is the mighty One coming back, and they recognize Him immediately.

Suddenly, however, there's a murmur, a buzz spreading through the thousands of heavenly onlookers, and one of them says to another, "There's the King—it's the King! But wait a minute . . . wait . . . who in the world is that with Him—that dirty, pitiful-looking ragamuffin straggling along beside Him?"

And Jesus, knowing their thoughts, says without blinking an eye, "The man is a sinner, saved by My grace. He is the first to enter My Kingdom with Me. There'll be others like him following behind."

Perhaps this is what is meant in Scripture: "The last shall be first" (Matthew 20:16).

And perhaps one day, as we stand amazed in His presence, we will finally understand what it really means to be *extravagantly loved by the King.*

Questions for Discussion

1. It is never too late to repent and run toward Jesus. The thief will be in Heaven enjoying all its glory alongside a saint who received Jesus at a very young age and did many things in His name while on Earth. Do you know someone, either a family member or friend, who does not know Jesus as Savior? What are you doing to be an example of what it means to know Him?

2. If you have been telling someone about Jesus but seemingly without any results, remember the thief on

the cross. Never give up. Why do you think Jesus so quickly accepted the man into His Kingdom?

3. Some say the foot of the cross is level ground. That means each of us is a soul equally in need of its healing power. Have you brought your heart to the foot of the cross? When and how did that happen? When we get to Heaven, the thief will be there. What, if anything, would you like to ask him?

Closing Thoughts

It is never too late to ask for forgiveness of sin. Jesus will welcome anyone *no matter what they have done* if they turn to Him. Why will He do this? Because He is the King . . . and He cherishes each of us with all the kingly love within Him.

Acknowledgments

I've been writing professionally for nearly forty years. Yet each time a book I've written is produced, the experience seems more wonderful than the last. So first and foremost, my thankfulness to God for allowing me to continue using my gifts and talents to honor Him in some small way.

Next, I'd like to thank the literary agency who gave birth to this publishing process in the first place—WordServe Literary, and specifically Greg Johnson. Many thanks, Greg, for guiding me on this journey!

That leads to the wonderful people at Salem Books of Regnery Publishing. Thanks to all of you for making this project so beautiful and complete. At the top of the list, a very special thanks to Publisher Tim Peterson, who encouraged and supported my endeavors every step of the way in order to get this book over the finish line!

To that end, Editorial Director Karla Dial added her wonderful editing skills, and Creative Director John Caruso worked his magic once more (this being the third cover he has done for my books at Regnery), plus others who helped perfect our project.

I'd also like to thank my little crew of people, who are also dear friends. I've relied upon them for every book I've written so far. My most excellent reader and sister-in-Christ, Brenda Holder, who once again helped me keep body and soul together with encouraging words and insights along the way. She also contributed a great personal story that's included in this book!

Next for technical support, Jim Wortham, who can do absolutely anything when it comes to computers, photos, files—all the things I'm not good at. Jim, your work is wonderful, and it helps make the written word come alive with color and images.

Now to the person I like to call "my" illustrator. The truth is, he is an incredible illustrator to so many: Bret Melvin. This makes the sixth book Bret has illustrated for me, sharing his wonderful drawing skills to give the reader that extra visual dimension. For this one, he also drew the lovely almond blossoms you see on the cover.

As always, I reserve dearest and most special thanks for my husband, Louis; his patience, particularly during deadlines, is beyond words. Truth be told, I couldn't do what I do without his support and encouraging words!

Notes

Author's Note

1. C. S. Lewis, *The Problem of Pain* (Grand Rapids, Michigan: Zondervan, 2001), 39.

Chapter 1: The Lesson of Simple Gestures

1. *Merriam-Webster Online*, s.v. "extravagant," https://www.merriam-webster.com/dictionary/extravagant.

2. Shelley Wachsmann, "Chapter 4: Galilean Seafaring in the Gospels," in *The Sea of Galilee Boat* (College Station, Texas: Texas A&M University Press, 2009), 112–19; Leen Ritmeyer, "Capernaum," Ritmeyer Archaeological Design, March 18, 2022, https://www.ritmeyer.com/2022/03/18/capernaum/; David Padfield, "Capernaum," 2017, 2, https://www.padfield.com/acrobat/history/Capernaum.pdf.

3. Wachsmann, "Chapter 4: Galilean Seafaring in the Gospels," 112; Ritmeyer, "Capernaum."

4. Gary M. Burge, "Fishers of Fish," *Christian History* 59, https://christianhistoryinstitute.org/magazine/article/fishers-of-fish.

5. Flavius Josephus, *The Wars of the Jews*, trans. William Whiston (Project Gutenberg, 2009), book III, chapter 10, paragraph 8, https://www.gutenberg.org/files/2850/2850-h/2850-h.htm.

Chapter 2: The Lesson of the Almond Tree

1. Toni Morrison, *Beloved* (New York: Vintage Books, 2004), 194.
2. "Almonds All around the World," Almond Board of California, https://www.almonds.com/why-almonds/global-history.
3. Daniel Zohary and Maria Hopf, *Domestication of Plants in the Old World: The Origin and Spread of Cultivated Plants in West Asia, Europe, and the Nile Valley* (Oxford: Oxford University Press, 2001), 186; G. Ladizinsky, "On the Origin of Almond," *Genetic Resources and Crop Evolution* 46 (1999): 143–47, https://doi.org/10.1023/A:1008690409554.
4. Vincent van Gogh, *Almond Blossom*, 1890, oil on canvas, 73.3 x 92.4 cm, Van Gogh Museum, Amsterdam, https://www.vangoghmuseum.nl/en/collection/s0176v1962.
5. FashionTV, "Dolce & Gabbana Spring/Summer 2014 FULL SHOW | Milan Fashion Week MFW | FashionTV," YouTube, October 7, 2013, https://www.youtube.com/watch?v=l6PaWaREPP0.
6. David Beaulieu, "How to Grow and Care for Almond Trees," The Spruce, June, 22, 2022, https://www.thespruce.com/how-to-grow-almond-trees-4779869.
7. "Market Profile: United States," Almond Board of California, February 2022, https://www.almonds.com/sites/default/files/2022-02/2022%20Market%20Profile_USA.pdf.
8. "Preparing Bees for Almond Bloom," *Almond Living Magazine*, February 6, 2017, https://www.almonds.com/why-almonds/almond-living-magazine/preparing-bees-almond-bloom.
9. "Pollinators and Farmer Win Big with Blooming Buffet for Bees," *Almond Living Magazine*, November 18, 2016, https://www.almonds.com/why-almonds/almond-living-magazine/pollinators-and-farmer-win-big-blooming-buffet-bees.
10. John R. W. Stott, *The Message of Romans* (Downers Grove, Illinois: InterVarsity Press, 1994), 36.
11. Ibid., 100.
12. Sue Surkes, "Erupting with Flowers before Spring, Almond Tree a Bounty of Jewish Symbolism," *The Times of Israel*, January 27, 2021, https://www.timesofisrael.com/erupting-with-flowers-before-spring-almond-tree-a-bounty-of-jewish-symbolism/.
13. "Almond Lifecycle," Almond Board of California, https://www.almonds.com/why-almonds/almond-lifecycle.
14. H. B. Tristram, *The Natural History of the Bible* (London: Society for Promoting Christian Knowledge, 1868), 332.

15. C. S. Lewis, *The Weight of Glory* (San Francisco, California: HarperSanFransisco, 1976), 183.

16. Jennifer Kornegay, "In a Nutshell: Different Nut Types, Explained," Feast and Field, December 6, 2021, https://feastandfield.net/read/grains-legumes-nuts/in-a-nutshell-different-nut-types-explained/article_7dc3c5f6-5235-11ec-8f06-4fd38e23b96d.html.

17. Zohary and Hopf, *Domestication of Plants in the Old World*, 133.

18. "Buds, Bees, and Bloom—Part 2: Bees," *Almond Living Magazine*, February 20, 2015, https://www.almonds.com/why-almonds/almond-living-magazine/buds-bees-and-bloom-part-2-bees.

19. Ladizinsky, "On the Origin of Almond."

Chapter 3: The Arts of Refining and Fulling

1. Mark Cartwright, "Gold in Antiquity," *World History Encyclopedia*, April 4, 2014, https://www.worldhistory.org/gold/.

2. Agatharchides of Cnidus, *On the Erythraean Sea*, ed. Stanley Burstein (London: The Hakluyt Society, 1990), book 5.

3. Diodorus Siculus, *Bibliotheca Historica*, trans. C. H. Oldfather (Cambridge, Massachusetts: Harvard University Press, 1933), book III, chapters 12–14, Loeb Classical Library.

4. J. H. F. Notton, "Ancient Egyptian Gold Refining: A Representation of Early Techniques," *Gold Bulletin* 7, no. 2 (June 1974): 52, https://doi.org/10.1007/BF03215038.

5. Ibid.

6. Diodorus Siculus, *Bibliotheca Historica*, 120–21.

7. Pliny the Elder, "Chapter 25: Eight Remedies Derived from Gold," in *Historia Naturalis, Book XXXIII: The Natural History of Metals*, http://data.perseus.org/citations/urn:cts:latinLit:phi0978.phi001.perseus-eng1:33.25.

8. Notton, "Ancient Egyptian Gold Refining," 54–6.

9. *The Hobbit: The Desolation of Smaug*, directed by Peter Jackson (Warner Bros. Pictures, 2013).

10. Elizabeth Wayland Barber, *Women's Work: The First 20,000 Years; Women, Cloth, and Society in Early Times* (New York: W. W. Norton & Co., 1995), loc. 2335, Kindle.

11. Bhavan Panghali, "Ancient Egyptian Clothing," *Egypt Quest*, https://egyptquest.wordpress.com/clothing/.

12. Ibid.

13. Ibid.

14. Ibid.

15. Brian Handwerk, "Feeling Overtaxed? The Romans Would Tax Your Urine," *National Geographic*, April 14, 2016, https://www.nationalgeographic.com/history/article/160414-history-bad-taxes-tax-day.
16. Charles Spurgeon, "The Sitting of the Refiner," presented at the Metropolitan Tabernacle, Newington, Spurgeon Gems, https://www.spurgeongems.org/sermon/chs1575.pdf.
17. Ibid.
18. Cartwright, "Gold in Antiquity."
19. Ibid.
20. Ibid.
21. Carole Engle Avriett, *Threads from Heaven* (Mountain Home, Arkansas: Borderstone Press, 2013), 69.

Chapter 4: A Lesson from Bread, Fish, and Eggs

1. M. Shahbandeh, "Per Capita Consumption of Eggs in the United States from 2000 to 2021," Statista, January 21, 2022, https://www.statista.com/statistics/183678/per-capita-consumption-of-eggs-in-the-us-since-2000/.
2. "Per Capita Seafood Consumption," IBIS World, Decmber 8, 2022, https://www.ibisworld.com/us/bed/per-capita-seafood-consumption/41/.
3. "Wheat Sector at a Glance: U.S. Wheat Use," Economic Research Service, U.S. Departent of Agriculture, updated October 26, 2022, https://www.ers.usda.gov/topics/crops/wheat/wheat-sector-at-a-glance/.
4. Nathan MacDonald, *What Did the Ancient Israelites Eat?* (Grand Rapids, Michigan: Wm. B. Eerdmans Publishing Company, 2008), 8.
5. Ibid., 19.
6. H. E. Jacob, "The Rivalry of the Grasses," in *Six Thousand Years of Bread: Its Holy and Unholy History* (New York: Skyhorse Publishing, 2014), 11; See also book 2 of the same publication: "Bread in the Ancient World."
7. Country Home Magazine, "The Rise and Fall of Ancient Bread," *Chicago Tribune*, February 9, 1986, https://www.chicagotribune.com/news/ct-xpm-1986-02-09-8601100787-story.html.
8. MacDonald, *What Did the Ancient Israelites Eat?*, 21.
9. Ibid.
10. Ibid.
11. Ibid.
12. National Geographic, "The Amazing Art of Bread Baking in Tajikistan | Short Film Showcase," YouTube, August 5, 2015, https://www.youtube.com/watch?v=XSocqMTohr4.
13. MacDonald, *What Did the Ancient Israelites Eat?*, 104.

14. Ibid., 8, 26, 29, 62.

15. Ibid., 58.

16. Ibid., 37–8.

17. Ibid., 38.

18. Leen Ritmeyer, "Harbours of the Sea of Galilee," Ritmeyer Archaeological Design, April 12, 2014, https://www.ritmeyer.com/2014/12/04/harbours-of-the-sea-of-galilee/.

19. Ilaria Gozzini Giacosa, *A Taste of Ancient Rome* (Chicago: University of Chicago Press, 1994), 27.

20. James Campbell, "Biblical Fishing 101: Reeling in the First Fishers of Faith," Loyola Press, https://www.loyolapress.com/catholic-resources/prayer/arts-and-faith/culinary-arts/biblical-fishing-101-reeling-in-the-first-fishers-of-faith/.

21. K. C. Hanson, "The Galilean Fishing Economy and the Jesus Tradition," *Biblical Theology Bulletin* 27, no. 3 (1997): 99–111, https://doi.org/10.1177/014610799702700304.

22. Joris Peters et al., "The Biocultural Origins and Dispersal of Domestic Chickens," *Proceedings of the National Academy of Sciences of the United States of America* 119, no. 24 (June 6, 2022): e2121978119, https://doi.org/10.1073/pnas.2121978119.

23. Jimmy Dunn, "The Diet of the Ancient Egyptians," Tour Egypt, http://www.touregypt.net/featurestories/diet.htm.

24. Maguelonne Toussaint-Samat, *A History of Food* (New York: Wiley-Blackwell, 2008), 323.

25. Marcus Gavius Apicius, *De Re Coquinaria (The Art of Cooking)*, ed. Sally Grainger (London: Prospect Books, 2006), 57.

26. Pliny the Elder, *Natural History* 388–89, Loeb Classical Library, https://doi.org/10.4159/DLCL.pliny_elder-natural_history.1938.

27. George Jennison, *Animals for Show and Pleasure in Ancient Rome* (Philadelphia: University of Pennsylvania Press, 2005), 106.

28. Apicius, *De Re Coquinaria,* 57.

29. Hannah Rice, "The Ancient Roman History of the Deviled Egg," Daily Meal, December 19, 2022, https://www.thedailymeal.com/1142998/the-ancient-roman-history-of-the-deviled-egg/.

30. Gordon D. Fee, *Listening to the Spirit in the Text* (Grand Rapids, Michigan: Wm. B. Eerdmans Publishing Company, 2000), 53.

Chapter 5: The Storehouses of Snow

1. Quote by W. A. Bentley in Mary B. Mullet, "The Snowflake Man," *The American Magazine* (1925), Snowflake Bentley, https://snowflakebentley.com/mary-mullet-article.

2.   Tiffany Means, "The Science of Snowflakes Explained," ThoughtCo., November 4, 2019, https://www.thoughtco.com/science-of-snowflakes-3444191.

3.   Chris Dolce, "Here's Why Snowflakes Can Be Large or Small," The Weather Channel, February 10, 2020, https://weather.com/safety/winter/news/2020-02-10-snowflake-size-difference-large-wet-small-dry.

4.   "Sastrugi," Cryosphere Glossary, National Snow and Ice Data Center, https://nsidc.org/learn/cryosphere-glossary/sastrugi.

5.   "Penitentes," European Southern Observatory, January 22, 2014, https://www.eso.org/public/australia/images/uhd_01_aec_166/?lang.

6.   Bjorn Carey, "Explaining Antarctica's Strange Megadunes," NBC News, July 25, 2005, https://www.nbcnews.com/id/wbna8701565.

7.   Robert J. Morgan, *The Red Sea Rules* (Nashville, Tennessee: Thomas Nelson, 2001), 82.

8.   *American Epic*, directed by Bernard MacMahon, aired June 6, 2017 on PBS, https://www.pbs.org/wnet/american-epic/.

Chapter 6: The Voice of the Lord

1.   "Your Voice and How It Works: Physiology," University of Minnesota Department of Otolaryngology–Head and Neck Surgery, https://med.umn.edu/ent/patient-care/lions-voice-clinic/about-the-voice/how-it-works/physiology.

2.   Ibid.

3.   "Your Voice and How It Works: Anatomy," University of Minnesota Department of Otolaryngology–Head and Neck Surgery, https://med.umn.edu/ent/patient-care/lions-voice-clinic/about-the-voice/how-it-works/anatomy.

4.   Dinesh Ramoo, "The Articulatory System," in *Psychology of Language* (British Columbia: BCcampus, 2021), https://opentextbc.ca/psyclanguage/chapter/the-articulatory-system/.

5.   João Aragão Ximenes Filho et al., "Length of the Human Vocal Folds: Proposal of Mathematical Equations as a Function of Gender and Body Height," *Ann Otol Rhinol Laryngol* 114, no. 5 (May 2005): 390–92, https://doi.org/10.1177/000348940511400510; Mao-Chang Su et al., "Measurement of Adult Vocal Fold Length," *The Journal of Laryngology & Otology* 116, no. 6 (June 2002): 447–49, https://doi.org/10.1258/0022215021911257.

6.   "Understanding Lightning: Thunder," National Weather Service, https://www.weather.gov/safety/lightning-science-thunder.

Chapter 7: The Wings of Eagles

1. Southwest Florida Eagle Cam, Dick Pritchett Real Estate, https://dickpritchettrealestate.com/southwest-florida-eagle-cam/.

2. "Ecology: Q&A about Bald Eagles with Peter Nye," New York Department of Environmental Conservation, JourneyNorth.org, https://journeynorth.org/tm/eagle/facts_ecology.html.

3. "Lesser Spotted Eagle," European Raptors, 2023, https://europeanraptors.org/lesser-spotted-eagle/.

4. Bernd-Ulrich Meyburg and Christiane Meyburg, "Annual Cycle, Timing and Speed of Migration of a Pair of Lesser Spotted Eagles (Aquila Pomarina)—A Study by Means of Satellite Telemetry," *Ostrich: Journal of African Ornithology* 89, no. 1 (December 2017): 67–8, http://www.raptor-research.de/pdfs/a_sp100p/a_sp150_PGE-06-063-085-Meyburg-Schreiadler.pdf.

5. Thomas Krumenacker, "The Migration of Lesser Spotted Eagle Aquila Pomarina, European Honey Buzzard Pernis Apivorus, Levant Sparrowhawk Accipiter Brevipes and White Stork Ciconia Ciconia over Northern Israel—A Balance over 30 Years of Counts," *CEPL Studies and Materials* (2013): 247–67, https://www.semanticscholar.org/paper/The-migration-of-lesser-spotted-eagle-Aquila-honey-Krumenacker/74c6f069b87cbaff12f2cd3438e0607870e926aa#citing-papers.

6. "Isaiah II: Biography of Isaiah, Map and Timeline," Loras College Library: Religious and Theological Sudies, https://library.loras.edu/c.php?g=100542&p=1075798.

7. Krumenacker, "The Migration of Lesser Spotted Eagle," 248–49.

8. "Raptors: Birth and Care of Young," Sea World Parks and Entertainment, https://seaworld.org/animals/all-about/raptors/care-of-young/.

Chapter 8: The Elusive Blue Dye

1. Hoakley, "The Dog, a Shell, and the Mark of High Office," The Eclectic Light Company, July 9, 2017, https://eclecticlight.co/2017/07/09/the-dog-a-shell-and-the-mark-of-high-office/.

2. Colin Schultz, "In Ancient Rome, Purple Dye Was Made from Snails," *Smithsonian Magazine*, October 10, 2013, https://www.smithsonianmag.com/smart-news/in-ancient-rome-purple-dye-was-made-from-snails-1239931/.

3. Kerry Sullivan, "Only the Roman Elite Could Wear Tyrian Purple to Keep the Peasants in Their Place," Ancient Origins, updated November 6, 2016, https://www.ancient-origins.net/history-ancient-traditions/only-roman-elite-could-wear-tyrian-purple-keep-peasants-their-place-021060.

4. Carole Engle Avriett, *Threads from Heaven* (Mountain Home, Arkansas: Borderstone Press, 2013), 52.
5. Sarah E. Bond, "The Hidden Labor behind the Luxurious Colors of Purple and Indigo," HyperAllergic, October 24, 2017, https://hyperallergic.com/406979/the-hidden-labor-behind-the-luxurious-colors-of-purple-and-indigo/.
6. Kari Rohde, "Origin of Ancient Blue Dye: Evidence from Time of King Solomon Found," Patterns of Evidence, July 28, 2017, https://www.patternsofevidence.com/2017/07/28/origin-of-ancient-blue-dye-evidence-from-time-of-king-solomon-found/; Ari Greenspan, "The Search for Biblical Blue," *Bible Review* 19, no. 1 (February 2003): https://www.baslibrary.org/bible-review/19/1/3; The Associated Press, "Long-Lost Biblical Blue Dye Believed Found in Ancient Textile," CBC News, December 31, 2013, https://www.cbc.ca/news/science/long-lost-biblical-blue-dye-believed-found-in-ancient-textile-1.2480125.
7. Clare Bruce, "An Encounter with God on the Moon: Astronaut Jim Irwin's Incredible Lunar Experience," Hope103.2, July 19, 2019, https://hope1032.com.au/stories/faith/2019/jesus-on-earth-is-more-important-than-man-on-the-moon-the-legacy-of-astronaut-jim-irwin/.
8. Vance Havner, *Day by Day* (Solid Christian Books, 2014), 47.
9. Jackie Green and Lauren Green-Mcafee, "The Praying Example of Susanna Wesley," Faith Gateway, https://faithgateway.com/blogs/christian-books/praying-example-susanna-wesley.
10. Ibid.
11. John A. Newton, *Susanna Wesley and the Puritan Tradition in Methodism*, 2nd ed. (London: Epworth, 2002), 98.
12. Susanna Wesley, *The Prayers of Susanna Wesley* (Grand Rapids, Michigan: Zondervan, 1984), 4–6.
13. Ibid.
14. Hoakley, "The Dog, a Shell, and the Mark of High Office."
15. Greenspan, "The Search for Biblical Blue."
16. Avriett, "The Blue Robe," in *Threads from Heaven*, 49–67.
17. Charles H. Spurgeon, *The Power in Prayer* (New Kensington, Pennsylvania: Whitaker House, 1996), 6.

Chapter 9: Mirrors for Glory

1. "Ancient Casting Practice," Copper Development Association, https://www.copper.org/education/history/60centuries/ancient/ancient.html.

2. Benjamin Galan, *Rose Guide to the Tabernacle* (Peabody, Massachusetts: Rose Publishing, 2008), 69–70.
3. "The History of Mirrors," MirrorHistory.com, 2023, http://www. mirrorhistory.com.
4. Ibid.
5. Ibid.
6. Stephanie Lowder, "The History of Mirror: Through a Glass, Darkly," Bienenstock Furniture Library, https://www.furniturelibrary.com/ mirror-glass-darkly/.
7. Mark Pendergrast, "'Mirror Mirror,'" *New York Times*, August 3, 2003, https://www.nytimes.com/2003/08/03/books/chapters/mirror-mirror.html.
8. "The History of Mirrors."
9. Juliet Le Page, "About Egyptian Dance," Egyptian Elementals, 2006, https:// www.eed.com.au/page/culture/about_egyptian_dance/essay/index.html.
10. Ibid.
11. Pendergrast, "'Mirror Mirror.'"
12. Alfred Edersheim, *The Temple: Its Ministry and Services* (Peabody, Massachusetts: Hendrickson Publishers, 1994), 32, 120–22.

Chapter 10: The Cedars of Lebanon

1. "The Cedars" MiddleEast.com, http://www.middleeast.com/thecedars.htm.
2. Hassan Salameh Sarkis, Elaine Larwood, and Françoise Hbeyka, "Cedars of the Shouf" in *The Cedars*, Ministry of Tourism of Lebanon, http://mot.gov. lb/Content/uploads/Publication/120806035723044~Cedre%20English.pdf.
3. Ibid., "Cedars of Bsharre."
4. Ibid., "The Cedars in History."
5. Ibid.
6. Ibid., "Cedars of Bsharre."
7. Lee Jagers, "Lessons from the Cedars of Lebanon," August, 18, 2014, https:// leejagers.wordpress.com/2014/08/18/lessons-from-the-cedars-of-lebanon/.
8. Ibid.
9. Ibid.
10. William McClure Thomson, "The Cedars of Lebanon," in *The Land and the Book* (New York: Harper & Brothers, 1859), 294–95.
11. Ibid., 295.
12. Ibid.

Chapter 11: The Veil, the Garment, the Thief (Part I)

1. Carole Engle Avriett, *The House* (Mountain Home, Arkansas: Borderstone Press, 2013), 34–5.
2. Ibid., 121.
3. Daniel M. Gurtner, "The Veil of the Temple in History and Legend," *Journal of the Evangelical Theological Society* 49, no. 1 (March 2006): 98–9, https://www.etsjets.org/files/JETS-PDFs/49/49-1/JETS_49-1_97-114_Gurtner.pdf.
4. David M. Levy, "THE VEIL: Christ Our Access to God," *Israel My Glory*, January/February 2023, https://israelmyglory.org/article/the-veil-christ-our-access-to-god-exodus-2631-35-3635-38/.
5. Charles Spurgeon, "The Rent Veil," presented at the Metropolitan Tabernacle, Newington, March 25, 1888, Spurgeon Gems, https://www.spurgeongems.org/sermon/chs2015.pdf.
6. Flavius Josephus, *The Wars of the Jews*, trans. William Whiston (Project Gutenberg, 2009), book VI, chapter 8, paragraph 3.
7. Randall Price, "Destruction of the Second Temple," in *Rose Guide to the Temple* (Peabody, Massachusetts: Rose Publishing, 2012), 407.

Chapter 12: The Veil, the Garment, the Thief (Part II)

1. Carole Engle Avriett, *Threads from Heaven* (Mountain Home, Arkansas: Borderstone Press, 2013), 58–60.
2. Ibid., 35–47.
3. C. S. Lewis, *The Weight of Glory* (New York: MacMillan Publishing, 1980), 4.
4. *The Robe*, directed by Henry Koster (20th Century Fox, 1953).
5. George Ryan, "Is This the Actual Robe of Jesus Christ?," uCatholic, May 30, 2017, https://ucatholic.com/blog/is-this-the-actual-robe-of-jesus-christ/.
6. Charles Spurgeon, "The Dying Thief in a New Light," presented at the Metropolitan Tabernacle, Newington, August 23, 1885, Spurgeon Gems, https://www.spurgeongems.org/sermon/chs1881.pdf.
7. Charles Spurgeon, "The Believing Thief," presented at the Metropolitan Tabernacle, Newington, April 7, 1889, Spurgeon Gems, http://www.spurgeongems.org/sermon/chs2078.pdf.